S0-BBC-958

CITYSPOTS
OSLO

Ann Burgess and Tom Burgess

Written by Ann Burgess & Tom Burgess
Updated by Lisa Govasli Nilsen

Published by Thomas Cook Publishing
A division of Thomas Cook Tour Operations Limited
Company registration No: 1450464 England
The Thomas Cook Business Park, 9 Coningsby Road
Peterborough PE3 8SB, United Kingdom
Email: sales@thomascook.com, Tel: +44 (0)1733 416477
www.thomascookpublishing.com

Produced by The Content Works Ltd
Aston Court, Kingsmead Business Park, Frederick Place
High Wycombe, Bucks HP11 1LA
www.thecontentworks.com

Series design based on an original concept by Studio 183 Limited

ISBN: 978-1-84157-885-9

Series Editor: Kelly Anne Pipes
Production/DTP: Steven Collins

Printed and bound in Spain by GraphyCems

Cover photography (Vigeland Sculpture Park) © Borchi Massimo/4Corners Images

CONTENTS

SYMBOLS KEY

The following symbols are used throughout this book:

ⓐ address   ☏ telephone   ⓦ website address
🕒 opening times   Ⓝ public transport connections

The following symbols are used on the maps:

𝒊	information office	▣	points of interest
✈	airport	◯	city
✚	hospital	◯	large town
🛡	police station	○	small town
▤	bus station	═	motorway
🚆	railway station	—	main road
Ⓜ	metro	—	minor road
✝	cathedral	—	railway
❶	numbers denote featured cafés & restaurants		

Hotels and restaurants are graded by approximate price as follows:
£ budget price   **££** mid-range price   **£££** expensive

▶ *Olso's City Hall*

Introduction

A trip to Oslo offers something for everyone. The city itself is
modern, while the surrounding scenery of the Oslofjord and
the wild woods and mountains of Nordmarka is beautiful.
Oslo can be visited at any time of year, although the warmest
and sunniest time to come is during the long days of summer.
The whole city seems to live outdoors at this time, with restaurants,
bars and museums keeping longer hours. Winter is also a lovely
time to visit, particularly for those who enjoy skiing (both downhill
and cross-country), luge, bobsleighing and skating. All of these
sporting activities are within easy distance of the city centre,
allowing you to spend your days in active pursuits and your
evenings absorbing Oslo's cultural treasures.

Oslo was once home to playwright Henrik Ibsen, composer
Edvard Grieg, violinist Ole Bull, artist Edvard Munch and sculptor
Gustav Vigeland. The city is proud of its heritage and has kept
alive its cultural traditions. And then of course there's the Vikings,
those adventurous bad boys of the Dark to Middle Ages who were
the first to scatter Norwegian traditions over a wide swath of
the globe. In later years they would be followed by the likes of
Amundsen and Heyerdahl, continuing the tradition of exploration
in a more socially responsible fashion.

Many of Norway's most important museums – more than
50 in total – are based in Oslo. Among the most notable are the
Munch Museum, Fram Museum and the Viking Ship Museum,
the Norwegian Folk Museum, Vigeland Sculpture Park, the Kon-Tiki
Museum, and the Holmenkollen ski jump, featuring the world's
oldest ski museum. Most of them are within walking distance

of the city centre, or just a few minutes away by a very effective public transport system.

Whatever your reasons for visiting Oslo, you won't be disappointed.

Akershus Slott has guarded Oslo harbour for centuries

When to go

SEASONS & CLIMATE

Oslo has four distinct seasons. Despite its northern latitude, the climate is quite moderate, owing to the effect of the Gulf Stream, which brings warm water from the Gulf of Mexico across the Atlantic and up the Norwegian coast. Summer temperatures average about 16°C (60°F), with highs that can reach 30°C (86°F), while winter temperatures average around 0°C (32°F), although they can go as low as -20°C (-4°F). You can expect about 80–90 mm (3–3½ in) of rain in the summer months, and about 40–50 mm (1½–2 in) in winter.

The main tourist season is from mid-June to mid-September. The summer season packs in a large number of festivals and other events, including plays and concerts, most of which are held outdoors. The city also has many parks and outdoor cafés to enjoy the long summer evenings. Visit ⓦ www.summeroslo.com for more information about Oslo's summer activities.

If you're into winter sports, especially skiing, then Oslo makes a great winter destination. The first snows fall in late November or early December, and the skiing season gets into full swing at Christmas time, lasting until April. Oslo has many kilometres of cross-country ski runs and 14 alpine ski slopes within the city limits, and many more within easy reach. For more information on skiing, visit ⓦ www.skioslo.com

ANNUAL EVENTS
March
Oslo International Church Music Festival Concerts are held in Oslo Cathedral and other churches within the city.
ⓦ www.oslokirkemusikkfestival.no

Barnas Holmenkollendag Kids aged 4–12 can participate in the world's largest ski race for children in Holmenkollen.
Ⓦ www.skiforeningen.no
World Cup Biathlon Some of the world's best athletes gather in Holmenkollen for Oslo's number one annual ski event.
Ⓦ www.skiforeningen.no

May/June
Labour Day (1 May) A very important public holiday. Events, parades and activities, all with a family fun theme, are held throughout the country.
Oslo Summer Festival Summer is celebrated in June with concerts, activities and traditional Norwegian food, all within the city centre.

● *Colourful Constitution Day celebrations*

Syttende Mai (Constitution Day) Norway's national day is celebrated across the country on 17 May. Activities include children's parades and other festivities.

Norwegian Wood Rock Festival Mid-June sees this three-day festival featuring mostly Norwegian performers, but several international stars are usually on the programme, too. Ⓦ www.norwegianwood.no

Oslo Gay & Lesbian Pride Week This festival takes place during the last week of June. Events include concerts, stand-up comedy, religious services, art exhibitions, photo workshops and bowling. Ⓦ www.skeivedager.no

Midsummer Night The evening of 21 June is the occasion for bonfires and celebrations throughout Norway.

July/August

Summer at the Folk Museum The open-air museum puts on family activities such as traditional Norwegian dancing and food, and play sessions with the museum's animals.

Norway Cup The world's largest international football tournament for 9–18s is held during the first week of August. Ⓦ www.norway-cup.no/uk

Oslo International Jazz Festival This major summer event takes place over a week in mid-August. All forms of jazz, from ragtime to rap, are showcased, with performers coming from all over the world to participate. Ⓦ www.oslojazz.no

Oslo Chamber Music Festival A mix of Norwegian and international musicians perform at various venues across the city in the middle of August. Ⓦ www.oslokammermusikkfestival.no

October/November

Ultima Contemporary Music Festival Held during the first two weeks of October, this festival collaborates with local museums and theatres to stage the latest in music, dance and drama. Ⓦ www.ultima.no

Oslo International Film Festival Movie lovers enjoy a combination of new trends and old classics in this 11-day event in November. Ⓦ www.oslofilmfestival.com

December
Nobel Peace Prize Award Parades and many other festivities are held in honour of the annual winner of the Nobel Peace Prize. Past performers have included Lionel Richie, John Legend, Andrea Bocelli and Katie Melua. Ⓦ www.nobel.no
Oslo Light Festival The beginning of Advent is celebrated with a variety of activities and entertainment in the city centre. Ⓦ www.osloarr.no/lysfest.html
Christmas Celebrations Christmas is celebrated with festivities and activities all over the city (see pages 12–13)

PUBLIC HOLIDAYS
New Year's Day 1 Jan
Maundy Thursday, Good Friday & Easter Monday
20–24 Mar 2008, 9–13 Apr 2009
Labour Day 1 May
Constitution Day 17 May
Ascension Day 1 May 2008, 21 May 2009
Whit Monday (Pentecost) 12 May 2008, 1 June 2009
Christmas 25 & 26 Dec

On Public Holidays, public transport runs to Sunday schedules, and banks, post offices and public buildings are closed. Many shops (but not generally restaurants) also close.

Christmas in Oslo

A very special time of year in Norway, Christmas, or *Jul*, was originally a pagan fertility feast before becoming a Christian holiday. Similarly, an imaginary Viking gnome called *Nisse*, who traditionally brought good luck to pagan farmers, has morphed into a modern-day Santa Claus in the form of *Julenissen*. The lighting of the city's official Christmas tree at University Square on Karl Johans Gate, on the first Sunday of Advent, heralds the start of the holiday season in Oslo. The ice skating rink in the city centre also opens at this time. For the whole of December Oslo is decked out in holiday lights and everyone is full of seasonal good spirits.

Pretty as the city centre may be, the holiday heart of Oslo is at the Norwegian Folk Museum on the Bygdøy Peninsula (see pages 90–9), which plays host to a charming Christmas fair. Here you can create a gift in Santa's workshop, join carollers in song and attend a service in the old Stave Church. Interspersed among the museum's historic buildings are market stalls filled with crafts, decorations and seasonal foods. You will also find traditional Christmas festivities at Bogstad Herregard in Frogner (see page 100). The main manor building is decorated in the style of the 19th century, while the gift shop sells a range of unusual gifts. It's also worth stopping off for a seasonal bite to eat at the café. In Oslo itself, a local sight to get into the holiday spirit is Bærums Verk, a 17th-century iron mill offering walks and horse-drawn sleigh rides. The old workers' houses have been converted into small shops selling hand-blown glass, pottery and woven and knitted items. You can even try your hand at creating your own Christmas decorations.

▶ *The Christmas Market at the Norwegian Folk Museum is worth a visit*

History

Although the history of Norway and its 'Norsemen' is a violent one, the history of Oslo itself is relatively quiet and peaceful. The Vikings had been plundering and pillaging for nearly 300 years by the time Oslo was founded in around 1000 by King Harald Hardråde. Roughly translated, Oslo means 'the pasture of the gods', from two Old Norse words, 'As', the Norse god, and 'lo', or 'field'.

By 1300 the city still had only 3,000 inhabitants, but it was nonetheless made the seat of the royal throne of King Haakon V, and consequently emerged as a centre of power. It was Haakon who started building Akershus Castle, which remains today. In 1349 the Black Death struck Norway, killing over half the country's population. Through royal marriages, Norway was joined to Denmark in 1380, with the Danes essentially ruling Norway for the next 400 years or so. Norway was a Catholic country until 1537, when the state religion became Evangelical Lutheran by royal decree. In 1624 Oslo was destroyed by fire. It was rebuilt by King Christian IV of Denmark, who renamed the city Christiania, after himself.

As a consequence of the Napoleonic wars, Norway was ceded to Sweden in 1814, with Christiania officially becoming its capital. Although it was under Swedish rule, Norway established a degree of democratic rule regarding domestic matters. For some reason, in 1877, the spelling of the city's name was changed to Kristiania, reverting to its original name of Oslo again in 1925.

In 1901 the home of the Nobel Peace Prize was moved to Oslo. After years of struggle for independence, the union with Sweden was dissolved peacefully in 1905 and Norway became a fully democratic constitutional hereditary monarchy. Norway stayed out of World War I, although it lost half of its merchant fleet in the struggle.

However, although Norway declared neutrality at the start of World War II, Germany invaded in 1940 and set up a puppet government under Vidkun Quisling. The exploits of the Norwegian resistance movement are legendary, and the execution of many Norwegian patriots took place in Akershus Castle. At the end of the war, the Germans surrendered to the Norwegian resistance movement at Akershus Castle, and Quisling was imprisoned there.

Following the war, Oslo and the rest of Norway prospered. A strong fishing industry and North Sea oil industry have kept the economy booming. Today Norway is one of the world's wealthiest nations per head of population. Although an active member of both NATO and the United Nations, to date an independently minded Norway has stayed out of the European Union with no immediate plans to join. The influx of immigrants from neighbouring European countries, Africa and Asia in recent years has given the country, and Oslo in particular, a more multi-cultural feel, with an increasingly international vibe.

ST HALLVARD

The patron saint of Oslo is St Hallvard, a young Norwegian of royal descent who sacrificed his life in a deed of valour nearly 1,000 years ago. According to legend, Hallvard tried to save a pregnant woman fleeing assailants who had accused her of theft. He rowed her out into the fjord, but the pursuers caught and killed them both, put a millstone around Hallvard's neck, and sank his body. However, the body rose to the surface with the millstone still in place. This miracle led to Hallvard's canonisation. Today St Hallvard, shown holding a millstone in his right hand, is the main icon in the city of Oslo's Coat of Arms.

Lifestyle

Modern-day Norwegians enjoy one of the highest standards of living in the world. But it wasn't always so: a little over 50 years ago Norway was one of the poorest countries in Western Europe. This changed following the discovery of oil in the North Sea in the late 1960s, resulting in a spectacular economic reversal of fortune.

The Norwegians are a conundrum. They can be simultaneously independent and yet heavily reliant on government social programmes. They are curious about the world, but reluctant to join the European Union. Eminently fair-minded, but wary of strangers, Norwegians frequently even see themselves as a bundle of contradictions. But one thing almost all Norwegians have in common is their love of the outdoors. They take the *allemannsretten* or 'every man's right' very seriously. This is the rule that allows complete public access to wilderness lands. During the very short summer months there is a frenetic urge to engage in any and all kinds of outdoor activities. Of course, they also participate in these sports in winter, but it's precisely the long winter months that make Norwegians long for the summer sun.

Norwegians are also among the best educated people on the planet. Education here is both compulsory and heavily funded. There is a wide range of programmes available to students, from traditional academic courses to vocational trades – and all of them are free. The citizens of Norway lead a very comfortable life. Although they are heavily taxed, they enjoy a vast range of benefits including free medical care, free university tuition, and a retirement pension. Because of the country's social programmes, with family allowances and generous parental leave policies, it is a good place to raise a family. The only fly in the ointment is the current problems associated with an ageing population.

Norway is a country with no external debt. Little wonder it can occasionally challenge world opinion, as in the case of its whaling policies. It will be interesting to see how Norway, having just marked its first centenary as a truly independent and sovereign nation, continues to evolve.

● *Like most northerners, Oslo's citizens make the most of every sunny day*

Culture

Oslo loves its museums, and with everything from art galleries to zoological gardens, they literally cover an A to Z of subjects. Architecture, children, literary heroes, skiers, sculptors and painters – they're all here. Still not enough? Don't worry: there are also historical museums, folk museums, geological museums and theatre museums. But these cultural repositories are more than just collections – they are a genuine reflection of Norwegian history, its life and its soul. The Viking Ship, Kon-Tiki and Fram Museum are authentic marvels. These are the actual ships that sailed astonishing distances and made incredible

discoveries: not replicas, the real thing. If you intend to sample as many of Oslo's museums as possible, invest in an Oslo Pass (see page 56).

Oslo is also a city of words. Literature has played a strong role in Norwegian culture. Few would dispute the impact and influence of Ibsen, Bjørnson or Sigrid Undset. Oslo is still a place that nurtures authors: Jostein Gaarder's powerful novel *Sophie's World* was a worldwide hit in the 90s.

Art, too, is a very powerful influence in everyday Oslo. Art is everywhere in the city – not just in galleries but also on the streets,

● *The Vikings left some ships behind at the Vikingskipshuset museum*

along the waterfront and in the parks. The sculpture park devoted to the work of Gustav Viegland and the museums dedicated to the work of Edvard Munch and other Norwegians artists help drive home the huge impact these artists had.

Music is big in Oslo. During the summer months concerts are held in parks and other open-air venues around the city. In winter it moves indoors to the concert halls and opera house. The city's contemporary music scene has greatly diversified in recent years. Young and talented musicians are beginning to receive national and international acclaim. One hip magazine has even taken to referring to 'the Oslo sound', a mix of jazz and electronica. Much of this expansion can be attributed to the spread of clubs, bars and new concert venues that enable both the musicians to express themselves and the public to hear them.

Oslo boasts memorable architecture. Contemporary additions such as the controversial Rådhuset (City Hall) find a comfortable place alongside the neo-classical lines of the Royal Palace. Elsewhere here you'll find chunks of living history and architecture combined in places like the old quarter in Gamlebyen, filled with centuries-old houses, well preserved and still occupied. It's a city crammed with works from both the past and the present, while leaving plenty of room for tomorrow's additions.

One tip: if you want to catch a glimpse of people wearing the bunad, or national costume, make sure you time your visit to coincide with a traditional festival or a wedding; otherwise you'll have to content yourself with viewing them in one of Oslo's historical museums.

▶ *Tall ships docked in Oslo's harbour*

MAKING THE MOST OF
Oslo

Shopping

Oslo can satisfy most shopaholics, with department stores, small boutiques and shops, antique emporiums, flea markets, open markets and tonnes of handicraft and souvenir shops. Most are open 09.00–17.00 Monday to Friday and until 15.00 on Saturday. Department stores are more generous, staying open until 20.00 on Friday and 18.00 on Saturday. Only during the holiday season will you find stores open on Sundays.

Traditional Norwegian souvenir shopping would have to include some knitwear, such as a brightly coloured, hand-knitted *lusekofte* sweater, mittens, gloves or a scarf. Knitting is a time-honoured tradition in Norway and at school both boys and girls are taught it. You might want to take a tip from Queen Sonja and present your friends with Norwegian pewter pieces – beer mugs, dishes and bowls are frequently decorated with traditional designs. For the child on your list you'll find lots of small cuddly items such as stuffed polar bears, furry seals and even some Norwegian trolls.

If you like your shopping compact, start in the city centre area near Karl Johans Gate. This pedestrian precinct is filled with familiar chain stores such as Benetton and H&M. If you prefer one-stop shopping in a department store or mall, the city centre area is home to Steen & Strøm, Paleet, Glassmagasinet and Byporten. Grünerløkka (see pages 84–9) is a young and hip area. Here, small independent stores are filled with clothes, pottery, handcrafts and even some used book and record stores. Young Norwegian designers frequently launch their products in the shops here.

In Majorstua (see pages 100–12) the streets of Bogstadveien and Hegdehaugsveien are a divine mix of both exclusive and mid-price

USEFUL SHOPPING PHRASES

What time do they open/close?
Når åpner/stinger den?
Nor orpner/stehng-er dehn?

How much is it?
Hvor mye kostet det?
Vor mew-yer koster deh?

I'd like to buy ...
Jeg kan få ...
Yeh kern for ...

stores. You could spend an entire day exploring these two streets – if your credit card holds up that long. Bygdøy Allé in Frogner (see page 100) is home to a good selection of modern interior design shops. Grønland (see pages 84–9), like Grünerløkka, almost defies description. The markets here are filled with vegetables and ethnic foods and the shops carry everything from fabrics to gold. Take some time to wander the streets of Grønlandsleiret and Smalgangen, where you will find many low-priced shops run by immigrants offering products from their home countries.

Eating & drinking

Traditional Norwegian food comes mostly from the sea. *Laks* (salmon), whether grilled, smoked or marinated, is very popular, as is *reker* (boiled shrimp), *sild* (herring), and *torsk* (cod). Boiled potatoes and other vegetables are normally served alongside meat or fish. You can expect to see pickled herring and *geitost* (a sweet brown goat's cheese) on breakfast buffets along with breads and cereals. A favourite Norwegian dessert is *moltebær syltetøy* (cloudberry jam), served warm with ice cream. *Eplekake* (apple cake) with fresh cream is also popular.

By most standards, Norwegian food is rather bland and heavy, although Oslo does have its share of excellent restaurants. For something a little different, you can try a reindeer, moose or whale steak. Vegetarians and vegans, admittedly, will find the city a challenge, as most menus are based on fish and meat.

At the bottom of the food chain are food wagons and street kiosks, where you can get hot dogs, hamburgers and soft drinks. Next up are the konditoris, or bakeries, which sell coffee, fresh pastries and sandwiches. Most have a few tables where you can sit and enjoy your food as you watch the street scene. For more substantial meals, try the kafeterias, which serve traditional, simple meals at reasonable prices. At the top end are kafes and restaurants: Oslo has a wide

PRICE CATEGORIES

The following price guide, used throughout the book, indicates the average price per head for a two-course dinner, excluding drinks. Lunch will usually be a little cheaper in each category.

£ 50–170Kr   **££** 170–250Kr   **£££** 250Kr+

variety of traditional and international restaurants, but the prices tend to be high.

Tipping is not required, but most people will round up the bill, and even leave a little extra if the service has been good.

On warm summer days, pick up some sandwiches, desserts and drinks at a konditori and head for Frognerparken or Vigeland Park for

● Oslo is a seafood-lover's paradise

a picnic. If you like seafood, you can buy freshly caught and cooked shrimps directly from the fishermen at the harbour. Enjoy shelling and eating them as you stroll along the harbour and buy a beer to wash them down with at a local café.

The national drink of Norway, if it had one, would be coffee, served strong and black. If you want to dilute yours with cream or add sugar you will have to ask for it. On the alcoholic side, most Norwegians consume a rather watery pilsner beer, or aquavit, a very strong and bitter spirit.

LUTEFISK

The dictionary defines *lutefisk* (pronounced 'lood-e-fisk') as 'stockfish that has been soaked in lye water, skinned, boned and boiled.' Lye is a strong alkaline liquid containing mainly potassium carbonate, obtained by leaching wood ashes with water. *Lutefisk* is normally served with butter, salt and pepper. The finished *lutefisk* usually has the consistency of gelatine and Norwegians traditionally serve it for Christmas. It's an acquired taste, and not for the weak of stomach.

The history of the dish dates back to Viking times and there are many legends surrounding its origin. Most tales involve dried cod that was subsequently caught in a fire. Water was used to put out the fire, and the dried fish was allowed to sit in the slush of the ash and the water. Someone then ate the fish that had been rehydrated with the resulting lye water, and that person apparently liked it. Anyone trying *lutefisk* for the first time has to wonder if that person was insane or just very hungry.

There are three types of drinking establishments in Oslo. The high-class bars with modern designs tend to be frequented by business people. The low-class, or 'brown' bars, serve the masses from dusty wooden establishments. The third class is chain or themed bars, such as Irish pubs, which are aimed mainly at tourists.

USEFUL DINING PHRASES

I would like a table for ... people, please
Et bord til ..., takk
Eht boor til ..., terk

May I see the menu, please?
Kan jeg få menyen, takk?
Kern yeh for men-ew-en, terk?

I am a vegetarian
Jeg er vegetarianer
Yeh ar veh-geh-ter-iahner

Where is the toilet (restroom) please?
Hvor er toalettene, takk?
Voor ar too-er-lehterner, terk?

May I have the bill, please?
Kan jeg få regningen, takk?
Kern yeh for rehg-ning-ehn, terk?

Entertainment & nightlife

Don't be fooled by first impressions. Underneath Oslo's outwardly conservative atmosphere is a healthy nightlife scene. There are countless cafés, bars and nightclubs to choose from and the vibe ranges from the ultra-trendy to the down-to-earth. Nightlife is an active ingredient of each area. From young and hip Grünerløkka to the more upscale Aker Brygge or the art-conscious cafés of Majorstua, you'll find plenty to keep you occupied. Oslo's nightlife is also very well dressed, and Norwegians expect you to be well shod and stylish. Save your grubby attire for the pub back home.

BARS & CLUBS

What's the difference between a café or a bar and a nightclub? In Oslo it can be hard to tell. Many cafés and bars that serve food during the day morph into a nightclub with a DJ playing music around 21.00–22.00 at night. This may also be the time when a cover charge appears. All restaurants, bars and nightclubs in Oslo, and the whole of Norway, for that matter, are smoke-free (see page 149), but many have outdoor tables during the summer, and in the winter lots of places provide outdoor heaters to keep their puffing patrons protected from the cold. Most bars and nightclubs are open until about 03.00, at least on Friday and Saturday nights.

MUSIC

Oslo ventures out at night for more than just a tipple. The city is home to a wide range of live stages and concert halls. This is, after all, the home country of Ibsen and Grieg and on almost any given night you'll be able to see one of their works being performed. Classical music is very much a part of Oslo's modern nightlife. The city boasts both a fine philharmonic symphony orchestra and opera company. You'll have plenty of opportunities to hear Grieg as well as more contemporary composers such as David Monrad Johansen, Geirr Tveitt, Fartein Valen and Pauline Hall. If you think there's nothing new in the world of opera, spend a Tuesday or Thursday evening at the **Underwater Pub** (ⓐ Dalsbergstien 4 ⓦ www.underwater.no), when students from the State School of Opera try out their skills. And, yes, part of the pub truly is under the sea.

🔺 *When the sun sets, Oslo's wide selection of bars and clubs brings the city to life*

Jazz, fusion and modern folk also have their place in Oslo. Norwegian saxophonist Jan Garbarek is a hot property, while the ethereal and haunting music of the Sami people has been experiencing a revival. Other must-listen-to artists include Aulu Gaup and Nils Aslak Valkeapaas. And, yes, you will still find traces of A-Ha, the Norwegian band of the 1980s that experienced a few fleeting moments in the world rock spotlight.

Traditional folk dancing and singing is also enjoying something of a renaissance and during the summer months there are plenty of festivals showcasing these activities. A century ago, when Norway was struggling to establish a cultural identity to accompany its newly acquired independence, there was a resurgence in traditional dances such as the polka, reinlender and mazurka. In 2005, as Norway celebrated its centenary, there was another wave of nationalism that once again brought these traditions to the forefront. Today troupes of *leikarringer* (folk dancers) appear in competitions all over the country.

LISTINGS

The *What's On in Oslo* brochure produced by the tourist office is a good place to find out what is happening where. *Streetwise*, a free publication, is another good source. Both of these are available in English.

● *Norway's National Theatre*

Sport & relaxation

Norwegians spend a lot of time outdoors, skiing in the winter and sailing, fishing and hiking in the summer. Most activities for visitors are linked to the outdoors.

WINTER SPORTS

Norway is the home of skiing. Rock carvings 4,000 years old show ancient Norwegians on skis. Fast forward to the 2006 Winter Olympics, and Norway came away with 19 medals.

All forms of skiing are popular in Norway – cross-country, downhill and ski jumping. Holmenkollen is the natural centre of winter activities in Oslo, being the host of both the World Cup Biathlon in March each year (see page 9), as well as family activities like Barnas Holmenkollendag (see page 9) and the Holmenkollen Ski Marathon. More information can be found at ⓦ www.skiforeningen.no.

● *All kinds of winter sports are very popular in Norway*

Tickets to all major sporting events are available at Norwegian post offices, by calling ☏ 815 33 133 or by logging on to ⓦ www.billettservice.no.

If you want to do it yourself, there are thousands of kilometres of ski trails in and around Oslo, as well as many alpine runs. In the summer, try the ski simulator at Holmenkollen. Other winter activities include ice skating and dog sledding.

OTHER SPECTATOR SPORTS

Football is also an important sport in Norway, with some 1,800 football clubs around the country. Oslo hosts the Norway Cup, the world's largest international football tournament for 9–18s, during the first week of August. More than 1,500 teams enter the competition. ⓦ www.norway-cup.no/uk

If you fancy a bet, Øvrevoll racetrack is just outside Oslo. Horse racing starts in April, and runs until December. There is also the Bjerke Trotting track, at Trondheimsveien, with racing on Wednesday evenings. **Racing** ⓦ www.ovrevoll.no, **Trotting** ⓦ www.bjerke.no

PARTICIPATION SPORTS & ACTIVITIES

Golf is popular in Norway, with several good courses in and around Oslo. For the less energetic, there are also several mini-golf courses. If you feel a Viking urge and want to ford the fjords, all manner of boats, from yachts to canoes and sea kayaks are available for rent. Just remember that plundering and pillaging are no longer allowed. **Yacht rental** ⓦ www.norwayyachtcharter.com, **Canoes & kayaks** ⓦ www.summeroslo.com

Gym bunnies take note: most major hotels have swimming pools, saunas and exercise/fitness rooms. There are also public pools and commercial spas and fitness clubs in Oslo.

Accommodation

Oslo can hardly be considered a budget location, and likewise its hotels are often considered expensive by visitors. But the city does have options to suit all budgets, and bargains can be had at weekends and during July and August.

HOTELS

City Hotel ££ Occupying several floors above a city building dating back to the 1800s, this is an intimate, simple hotel with a very quiet atmosphere. ❸ Skippergaten 19 ❶ 22 41 36 10 Ⓦ www.cityhotel.no Ⓝ Tram: 19 to Kirkegata

Residence Kristinelund ££ This friendly B&B in an atmospheric turn-of-the-century house is located in a posh residential area off Bygdøy Allé. There are 19 airy rooms (with shared bathrooms), some with balconies. ❸ Kristinelundsveien 2 ❶ 40 00 24 11 Ⓦ www.kristinelund.no Ⓝ Bus: Olav Kyrres Plass

Thon Hotel Munch ££ A basic hotel, reasonably priced and in a central location that's surprisingly quiet. Some rooms are accessible for visitors with mobility problems. ❸ Munchs Gate 5 ❶ 23 21 96 00 Ⓦ www.thonhotels.no/munch Ⓝ Tram: Tinghuset; T-Bane: Jernbanetorget

PRICE CATEGORIES
Hotel ratings in this book are based on cost of a double room for one night, not including breakfast (unless otherwise stated).
£ 150–600Kr **££** 600–1,000Kr **£££** 1,000Kr+

larion Collection Hotel Gabelshus ££–£££ A 15-minute walk from the centre in a quiet, upmarket neighbourhood, this well-furnished hotel offers good value for the price, with free parking and morning and evening buffets. Gabels Gate 16 ☎ 23 27 65 00 ⓦ www.gabelshus.no Ⓝ Tram: 10

Rica Helsfyr Hotel ££–£££ This modern hotel in a rural location is just a short distance from the T-bane. Well equipped and a good choice for those who don't want the hustle and bustle of city life. ⓐ Strømsveien 108 ☎ 23 06 78 78. ⓦ www.rica.no Ⓝ T-Bane: Helsfyr

Thon Hotel Linne ££–£££ A modern business and conference hotel located only 15 minutes by car or T-bane from downtown Oslo. There's a licensed bar, parking and breakfast are included in the price, and the airport bus express also stops nearby. ⓐ Statsråd Mathiesens vei 12 ☎ 23 17 00 00 ⓦ www.linne.no Ⓝ Bus: 60 to Linne Hotell

Thon Hotel Terminus ££–£££ A modern, well-equipped hotel within walking distance of the main railway station. Dinner included in the price, Monday to Thursday. Disabled access. ⓐ Stenersgata 10 ☎ 22 05 60 00 ⓦ www.thonhotels.no/terminus Ⓝ T-Bane/Tram/Bus: Jernbanetorget

Thon Hotel Vika Atrium ££–£££ An efficient, business-oriented hotel on the edge of the Aker Brygge area, close to transport, shops and restaurants. A fitness room and sauna are available. ⓐ Munkedamsveien 45 ☎ 22 83 33 00 ⓦ www.thonhotels.no/vikaatrium Ⓝ T-Bane: Nationaltheateret

Best Western Bondeheimen Hotel £££ A traditional hotel that, despite modernisation, has kept its Norwegian country feel. Business facilities and a Norwegian restaurant are also on site. ⓐ Rosenkrantz Gate 8 ⓣ 23 21 41 00 ⓦ www.bondeheimen.com ⓝ Tram: Prof. Aschehougs Plass; T-Bane: Stortinget

Clarion Collection Hotel Savoy £££ This centrally located hotel with bright modern rooms is a popular meeting place for travellers and locals alike. ⓐ Universitetsgata 11 ⓣ 23 35 42 00 ⓦ www.choice.no ⓝ Tram: 11, 17, 18 to Tullinløkka; T-Bane: Nationaltheateret

First Hotel Millennium £££ Atmospheric first-class hotel, right in the heart of Oslo near the Parliament building, Akershus Fortress and Karl Johans Gate. ⓐ Tollbugata 25 ⓣ 21 02 28 00 ⓦ www.firsthotels.no ⓝ Tram: 12, 13, 19 to Kirkegata

Norlandia Karl Johan Hotel £££ Smartly renovated hotel that has a long tradition of offering comfortable lodgings and boasts a central location, right on Karl Johans Gate. ⓐ Karl Johans Gate 33 ⓣ 23 16 17 00 ⓦ www.norlandia.no/karljohan ⓝ Bus: Wessels Plass; T-Bane: Nationaltheateret

Radisson SAS Plaza Hotel £££ The Radisson's soaring dramatic exterior of tinted blue glass with a needle summit belies its intimate and well-decorated rooms. The views from the upper floors are astonishing (it is, after all, Northern Europe's tallest hotel). A fitness centre with sauna and pool are further draws. ⓐ Sonja Henies Plass 3

⊙ *Oslo's Grand Hotel*

🕿 22 05 80 00 🌐 www.plaza.oslo.radissonsas.com Ⓝ T-Bane:
Jernbanetorget (Oslo S): Tram: 11, 13, 17 to Brugata

Rica Grand Hotel £££ With its landmark mansard roof and copper
tower, Oslo's premier hotel has been an integral part of daily life
since 1874. Henrik Ibsen, Edvard Munch, Dwight Eisenhower and
Henry Ford have all stayed here. Ⓐ Karl Johans Gate 31 🕿 23 21 20 00
🌐 www.grand.no Ⓝ Bus: Wessels Plass; T-Bane: Nationaltheateret

Rica Victoria Hotel £££ A centrally located hotel, within walking
distance of many of Oslo's main tourist attractions and widespread
shopping possibilities. Business facilities and internet access
on site. Ⓐ Rosenkrantz Gate 13 🕿 24 14 70 00 🌐 www.rica.no
Ⓝ T-Bane: Stortinget

Thon Hotel Cecil £££ Located next to the Parliament in the city
centre, just a few steps from Karl Johans Gate, this hotel has large,
well-equipped rooms with internet access. Ⓐ Stortingsgata 8
🕿 23 31 48 00 🌐 www.thonhotels.no/cecil
Ⓝ T-Bane: Nationaltheateret

Thon Hotel Europa £££ A casual and informal hotel within easy
reach of the city centre. Guests have use of a nearby fitness facility.
Ⓐ St Olavs Gate 31 🕿 23 25 63 00 🌐 www.thonhotels.no/europa
Ⓝ T-Bane: Nationaltheateret; Tram: Tullinløkka

Thon Hotel Opera £££ Within easy reach of Oslo Central Station.
The decor is modern and somewhat spartan, but the facilities are
good and include a fitness centre with sauna and a coffee shop.
Disabled access. Ⓐ Christian Frederiks Plass 5 🕿 24 10 30 30

Ⓦ www.thonhotels.no/opera Ⓝ T-Bane: Jernbanetorget (Oslo S);
Tram: Jernbanetorget

Thon Hotel Stefan £££ Newish hotel that's well known for its
popular lunch buffet. Room features include internet access,
and non-smoking rooms are available. Ⓐ Rosenkrantz Gate 1
Ⓣ 23 31 55 00 Ⓦ www.thonhotels.no/stefan Ⓝ Tram: Tinghuset;
T-Bane: Stortinget

HOSTELS
Anker Hostel £ This place has an international atmosphere and
a spit-and-polish approach to cleanliness. Most rooms have at least
four beds, and some have six. Facilities include laundry, a kitchen and
a small bar. Note that linen is not included. Ⓐ Storgata 55 Ⓣ 22 99 72 00
Ⓦ www.ankerhostel.no Ⓝ Tram/Bus: Hausmannsgate

Oslo Hostel Rønningen YMCA £ A cheap option with singles
and doubles as well as rooms with up to four beds. The hostel
only operates during the summer months and fills up quickly,
so book well in advance. Breakfast is included; linen isn't.
Ⓐ Myrerskogveien 54 Ⓣ 21 02 36 00 Ⓦ www.oslohostel.com
Ⓝ Tram: 10, 12 to Disen; Bus: 56 to Solheimsskogen

Oslo Vandrerhjem Haraldsheim £ Most of the rooms at this
centrally located hostel have four beds, but some double rooms
are available. There are laundry and kitchen facilities on site;
linen is not provided. Breakfast included. Ⓐ Haraldsheimvn 4
Ⓣ 22 22 29 65 Ⓦ www.vandrerhjem.no Ⓝ Tram: 17 to Sinsenkrysset;
Bus: 31, 32 to Sinsenkrysset: T-Bane: Sinsen

THE BEST OF OSLO

If you have only a limited amount of time in Oslo, here are ten experiences you shouldn't miss.

TOP 10 ATTRACTIONS

- **Holmenkollen Ski Jump** Oslo's most frequently visited attraction (see pages 100–2). Here you can hike to the top to get a breathtaking view of the city, and the course that world class ski-jumpers attempt to conquer.

- **Norwegian Folk Museum** (see page 94). A lovely outdoor museum with the largest collection of cultural history in Norway.

- **Akershus Castle** This centuries-old fortress is still used for state occasions and contains the Resistance Museum, which gives a startlingly forthright account of the German occupation of Norway (see pages 62–6).

- **Kon-Tiki Museum** Thor Heyerdahl mesmerised the world with his balsa-log raft voyages across the Pacific Ocean in 1947. The raft itself is on permanent display along with artefacts from that voyage and the papyrus boat, the Ra II (see page 93).

- **Vikingskipshuset (Viking Ship Museum)** The Viking ships on display – the Gokstad, Tne and Oseberg, all dating from 800–900 – are the best-preserved in any museum (see page 97).

- **Rådhuset (City Hall)** The site of the presentation of the Nobel Peace Prize is either a superb or remarkably ugly piece of architecture, depending on your taste. However you see it, it's certainly dramatic (see pages 69–70).

- **Munch Museet** Edvard Munch's body of work is well represented here, along with the works of many other Norwegian artists (see pages 85–6).

- **Vigeland Sculpture Park** Located in Frogner Park, this is one of Oslo's most remarkable attractions. The 212 dramatic bronze, granite and iron sculptures of Gustav Vigeland depict his vision of humanity in all its forms (see page 104).

- **Nasjonalgalleriet (National Gallery)** Only a short walk from Karl Johans Gate is one of Norway's largest collections of important pieces of art, design and architecture. Be sure to take a stop in The Edvard Munch Hall to see the world famous *Skrik* (*The Scream*) (see pages 73–4).

- **Aker Brygge** Once an active shipyard, this abandoned industrial area has been transformed into one of Oslo's most attractive waterfront areas, filled with shops and restaurants. It's a perfect place to sip a glass of wine and view the fortress of Akershus across the water (see page 62).

The harbour, the perfect spot to relax

Suggested itineraries

Here's a quick guide to seeing the best of Oslo, depending on the time you have available.

HALF-DAY: OSLO IN A HURRY

If you only have half a day, put on some comfy shoes for a walk through the centre to take in some of Oslo's top sights. Starting at the main railway station, Oslo S, walk west along Karl Johans Gate towards the Royal Palace (Slottet). The first building on the right is Oslo Domkirke (Cathedral). As you continue along Karl Johans Gate you will come to Stortinget, the home of the Norwegian parliament. Turn left onto Kongens Gate, where you will find the Norwegian Architecture Museum. Turn left again onto Revierstredet where you will see Engebret Café, Oslo's oldest eatery. Turn right onto Kirkegata, and you will pass the Museum of Contemporary Art (entrance on

◆ *Aker Brygge is the perfect place to spend a sunny day*

Myntgata). At the end of Kirkegata, you will come to a drawbridge which will take you over Kongens Gate and into Akershus Castle. Work your way north through the fortress and exit through a gate onto Akersgate. Turn right onto Rådhusgata to see Christiania Torv (Square) and the Theatre Museum. Retrace your steps and continue west on Rådhusgata until you come to the Rådhuset (Town Hall). Walk around the Rådhuset, through Fridtjof Nansens Plass and onto Roald Amundsens Gate, where you will find the National Theatre. Cross Karl Johans Gate and you will be beside the University. Turn left on Kristian IVs Gate which will take you past the National Art Gallery and the History Museum. At Frederiks Gate you can cross into the gardens of the Royal Palace. Work your way south through the Royal Palace complex until you emerge onto Drammensveien and go west. Passing the Ibsen Museum, turn left onto Huitfeldts Gate and left again onto Cort Adelers Gate. This will take you into Aker Brygge. Find a nice restaurant on the waterfront to enjoy lunch and a cold Norwegian beer – you deserve it.

1 DAY: TIME TO SEE A LITTLE MORE

A whole day gives you time to explore one or two of the sights on the half-day walk in more depth. Alternatively, follow the half-day tour in the morning and after lunch take a ferry from Aker Brygge to Bygdøy, getting off at Bygdøynes. As you alight, you will see the Gjoa. Just past the Gjoa is a large plaza, onto which three major maritime museums face: the Fram Museum, the Kon-Tiki Museum, and the Norwegian Maritime Museum. After exploring at least one of these museums, it is worth the extra 1 km ($^1/_2$ mile) walk to perhaps the best of them all: follow Bygdøynesveien, turn right onto Langviksveien and left onto Huk Aveny, which will bring you to the entrance of the Viking Ship Museum. From this museum, retrace your steps to

Langviksveien. From here, if you still have time, you can continue north to the Norwegian Folk Museum. From the Folk Museum, continue north on Langviksveien, turn right on Museumsveien, and left onto Huk Aveny. At the end of Huk Aveny, you can catch a ferry back to Aker Brygge and another beer.

2–3 DAYS: TIME TO SEE MUCH MORE

The half-day and one-day sightseeing walks can easily be expanded into two or three days if some of the museums take your fancy. But if not, there's still plenty more to pack in. Other sights worth visiting include the Munch Museum, the Holmenkollen Ski Jump, Vigeland Park and Museum, and Gamlebyen. Oslo also has many smaller museums dedicated to just about anything you can imagine. Spend at least one evening wining and dining with the locals in Grünerløkka.

LONGER: ENJOYING OSLO TO THE FULL

If you have lots of time, you can easily spend several more days taking in what Oslo has to offer. If you feel a need to get away from the city, however, you can discover Norway outside Oslo. Perhaps the best way is to take the 'Norway in a Nutshell' tour. It can be done in two days (Oslo to Bergen), but you may want to spend up to a week to really get a feel for the country, by adding loops to Stavanger and Sognefjord. Other options include one- or two-day trips down the east coast of Oslofjord to Drøbak, Fredrikstad and Halden – by car, bus, train or ferry – or a two- or three-day excursion north to Lillehammer, Røros and Trondheim. Perhaps the best of all for a truly get-away-from-it-all feeling is the coastal cruise north from Bergen. You can go as far north as time and funds allow.

▶ *The Fram Museum at Bygdøy is well worth a visit*

Something for nothing

Although Oslo can't be considered the most expensive city in the world, the cost of living here is high, and most visitors are pleased to find out that there are plenty of things for them to enjoy for free. Below are some suggestions.

Botanical Gardens Take tram 13 or 17 and get off at the Botanical Gardens for a relaxing day among the beautiful collection of Norwegian and foreign plants. ⓐ Sars Gate 1 ⓣ 22 85 16 30

Astrup Fearnley Museum of Modern Art is home to an extensive collection of post-war art from Norwegian and international artists (see page 72).

Forsvarmuseet (Norwegian Armed Forces Museum) This museum traces Norway's military history from the Vikings to the 1950s (see page 67). Dioramas, models and historical objects are used to recreate this fascinating segment of history.

Oslo City Museum Set in the distinguished Frogner Manor (see pages 104–6), the surroundings themselves are worthy of a visit. The city's history is displayed in models, photographs, objects and paintings. The museum also offers historical town walks.

Vigeland Park Norway's most visited attraction is filled with more than 200 sculptures by noted artist Gustav Vigeland, who also designed the layout of the park (see page 104).

Akebakken Luge If the weather is right (snow on the ground) and you're feeling brave, pay a trip to this popular luge track. Even if you don't have your own sled, it's fun to watch. ⓐ Akebakken, 8 km (5 miles) from the city centre. ⓝ Bus: 56 to Akebakken.

Skating Take a spin on the ice during the winter months at one of Oslo's many outdoor rinks. The skating is free, but unless you've brought your own blades you'll have to rent skates. Most rinks are open every day from December to March.

ⓞ *Gustav Vigeland's sculpture theme park is an unforgettable sight*

When it rains

It's raining? Throw on your best cape and deerstalker hat and head to Æreslunden, Oslo Cathedral's Memorial Graveyard, and contemplate the loss of such notable figures as Edvard Munch and Henrik Ibsen. If you don't want to get wet, then Oslo has a vast range of museums for every taste that will absorb your time. Or follow up some of these other leads.

Bærums Verk is a delightful collection of buildings from 1610 that are filled with craft shops and restaurants. You may have to dodge the raindrops between the buildings but it's a good way to spend a few hours on a dreary day sipping hot chocolate and admiring the work of artisans. It takes on a festive air at Christmas (see pages 12–13).

When only a mall crawl will satisfy your need to be active but remain dry, head to the city centre for the Byporten Center (see page 77), next to Central Station, or Steen & Strøm, also in the city centre, an inspired collection of shops offering everything from clothes and books to perfumes, furniture, shoes and toys.

● *Oslo gets a lot of rain, but luckily there's plenty to see and do indoors*

On arrival

TIME DIFFERENCE
Oslo's clocks follow Central European Time (CET). During Daylight Saving Time (end Mar–end Oct), the clocks go forward one hour.

ARRIVING
By air
Oslo International Airport is located at Gardermoen, about 50 km (30 miles) north of the city. It opened in 1998 and is still looking very new, with facilities that include banks, ATMs, currency exchange, restaurants, tourist information desks, newsagents, gift shops and a pharmacy. The airport is usually busy, and the layout requires some long walks, so allow extra time in planning your schedule on

---

IF YOU GET LOST, TRY ...

Excuse me, do you speak English?
Unnskyld meg, snakker du engelsk?
Unshewl mey, snerkur doo ehng-erlsk?

How do I get to ...?
Hvordan kommer jeg til ...?
Voordern kommer yeh til ...?

Can you show me on my map?
Kan du vise meg på kartet?
Kern doo veesur meh po kertur?

---

arriving or departing. If you haven't acquired any Norwegian kroner (Kr) before leaving your home country, make sure you get some at the airport, as few local businesses accept foreign currencies.

From the airport, high-speed trains (Flytoget) go to Oslo S, the city's central railway station. The trains run every ten minutes, and take about 20 minutes to get there. The fare is 160Kr. There are also express buses to Oslo S operated by SAS Transport Service. The buses leave every 20–30 minutes, and travel time is about 40 minutes. The fare is 130Kr one way or 220Kr return. Taxis are available outside the arrivals area, but the fare to central Oslo is expensive, starting at 650Kr. There are desks for all major car rental companies at the airport.

Oslo is served by most international airlines. Domestic flights to other parts of Norway also leave from Gardermoen.

Flytoget Ⓦ www.flytoget.no

Oslo International Airport ❶ 64 81 20 00 Ⓦ www.osl.no

SAS Transport Service buses Ⓦ www.flybussen.no/oslo

Sandefjord Airport Torp is located 110 km (70 miles) southwest of Oslo, and is now Norway's second largest international airport. Some low-cost airlines are now using this airport as a second gateway to Oslo. The Torp Express bus service connects with some arriving flights, and takes about two hours to get to the main bus station in Oslo. Since this is not valid for all flights it is wise to call in advance on ❶ 67 80 04 70. It is also possible to take a train from Sandefjord to Oslo, but you will need to take a local bus or taxi to the Sandefjord Railway Station. By car, simply take Highway E16 from the airport to Oslo. All the major car hire companies are represented here, too.

Sandefjord Airport Torp Ⓦ www.torp.no

By rail

Oslo Sentralstasjon (Central Station) is simply called Oslo S, and is located at the eastern end of Karl Johans Gate near the city centre. Oslo S is the main transportation link in the city. Trains from continental Europe, from other parts of Scandinavia and from other cities in Norway all arrive here, as do the buses and trains from the airports. The main bus station is adjacent to Oslo S and can be reached by an overhead walkway.

Oslo S has many facilities, including an InterRail centre with showers, plus an efficient tourist information centre that can provide maps, information, and assist with currency exchange, hotel reservations and also sell you an Oslo Card. There is also a post office, an internet café, restaurants and bars inside the station. Taxis, buses, and trams are just outside the station. There is also an underground (T-bane) station.

The adjacent shopping centre, Byporten, can be accessed directly from the main gallery. On the southern side is Østbanehallen, the old part of the station, which has been converted into a small shopping arcade. ⓐ Jernbanetorget 1 ⓦ www.nsb.no ⓛ 06.00–23.15 Mon–Fri, 06.30–23.15 Sat, 07.00–23.15 Sun

By road

Bussterminalen, the main bus station, is situated on the north side of Oslo's central railway station, which makes transfers between the two very easy. All local bus services, as well as those arriving from further afield, arrive and depart from here. ⓐ Schweigaards Gate 8

Cars must pay a 15 to 25Kr toll each time they enter Oslo. Oslo has many one-way streets, which can make driving around confusing, although traffic congestion is not a problem. There is lots of parking in the centre of the city, but it can be expensive. There is metered parking on the streets; it's expensive during business hours (up to 50Kr per hour) but normally free during other times. There are also plenty of parking garages, but they can cost up to 200Kr per day. The Oslo Pass gives free parking in municipal car parks.

By water

International ferries arrive and depart from two piers. Vippetangen pier is just below Akershus Castle, and Hjortneskaia pier is adjacent to Aker Brygge. Both are on the waterfront close to the centre of Oslo.

Ferries to other parts of the Oslo fjords leave from Vippetangen. Ferries to the Bygdøy Peninsula leave from Rådhusbrygge 3 in front of the Rådhus (City Hall). These ferries only run in the warmer months – mid-April to early October.

FINDING YOUR FEET

Finding your feet in Oslo is easy. This is a user-friendly city, and the people are open and generous. Many of the attractions and hotels are close enough to the city centre that they can be reached on foot, and the efficient public transport system gives access to those that

TRAFIKANTEN

Trafikanten is an information office for public transportation in and around Oslo. It is located next to Oslo S at Jernbanetorget. The office has timetables for trains, buses, trams, the underground (T-banen), and ferries that operate in Oslo, the greater Oslo area, and Central Eastern Norway. ⓐ Jernbanetorvet 1 ⓘ 81 50 01 76 ⓦ www.trafikanten.no ⓛ 07.00–20.00 Mon–Fri, 08.00–18.00 Sat & Sun

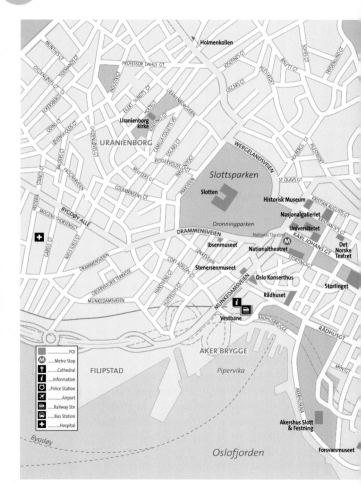

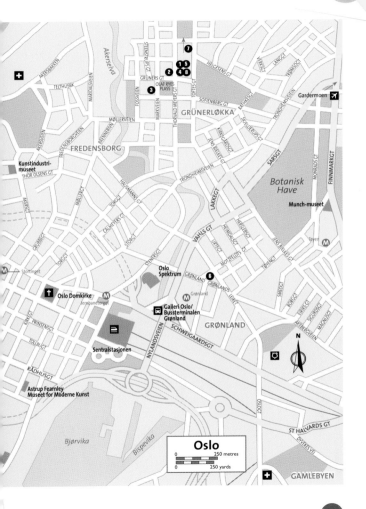

Oslo

| 0 | | | | 250 metres |
| 0 | | | | 250 yards |

can't. Crime is not a worry if you take the normal precautions. However, prices and taxes are high in this city, so be prepared to pay for everything from road tolls to toilets. Be warned that many attractions close on a Monday – this might be a good time to head out of the city or to the shops.

ORIENTATION

Karl Johans Gate is the main street in central Oslo. It runs east–west, with Oslo S at the eastern end and the Royal Palace at the western end. Most hotels, as well as many of the city's attractions, are within a 15-minute walk of Karl Johans Gate. The waterfront, Aker Brygge,

OSLO PASS

If you intend to visit a number of attractions in a short period of time, you should invest in the Oslo Pass. It gives free admission to most museums and attractions, free travel on public transport (except night buses), free parking in municipal car parks, and discounts on sightseeing and car rental and at restaurants and amusement parks. The card is available in 24-, 48-, and 72-hour versions, and can be purchased for individual adults and children, or as a family pass (two adults, two children). It is sold at Tourist Information Centres, most major hotels, some Narvesen kiosks, at Trafikanten (see page 53), or through the net Ⓦ www.visitoslo.com. An information booklet outlining all the benefits comes with the Oslo Pass.

An Oslo Package is also available, which includes hotel accommodations as well as the Oslo Pass.

Rådhuset and Akershus Castle are just a few blocks south of Karl Johans Gate. Most streets, especially those in central Oslo, follow a standard grid pattern.

GETTING AROUND
Public transport

Getting around the city is quite easy. The centre part of the city is easily and safely walkable, and considering the Norwegians' penchant for hiking, this is the preferred mode of transport. If you want to travel a little further afield, the public transport system, consisting of buses, trams and T-bane (metro, subway), is very efficient. Tickets for single trips cost 22Kr if purchased in advance, or 30Kr if purchased from the driver. Advance tickets can be purchased from 7-eleven stores, Narvesen kiosks, and from Trafikanten. Daily passes cost 60Kr. Multi-day passes are also available. The Oslo Pass gives free transport during the daytime and evening, but not late at night. Note that there is an honour system regarding tickets, and the fine for travelling without a ticket is a hefty 750Kr.

Taxis

Taxis are easy to find and use in Oslo. They are safe and clean, but can be expensive. The fare starts at up to 56Kr plus up to 24Kr per kilometre. It's cheaper to flag a taxi rather than to call one, as the flag drops when a called taxi is dispatched and you can owe a small fortune before the taxi even picks you up.

CAR HIRE

Rental cars are readily available, and most major rental agencies are represented at both the airport and in Oslo. However, rental car rates are very high, and car insurance is extra. Some local rental agencies

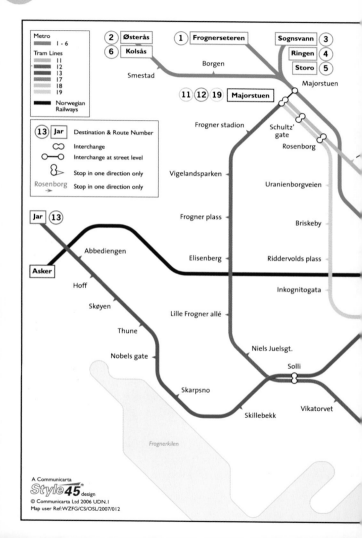

Metro
1 - 6
Tram Lines
11
12
13
17
18
19
Norwegian Railways

13 Jar Destination & Route Number
∞ Interchange
○—○ Interchange at street level
○—▷ Stop in one direction only
Rosenborg Stop in one direction only

2 Østerås
6 Kolsås
1 Frognerseteren
3 Sognsvann
4 Ringen
5 Storo

Borgen
Smestad
Majorstuen

11 12 19 Majorstuen

Frogner stadion
Schultz' gate
Rosenborg

Vigelandsparken
Uranienborgveien

Jar 13

Frogner plass
Briskeby

Abbediengen
Elisenberg
Riddervolds plass

Asker
Inkognitogata

Hoff
Skøyen
Lille Frogner allé

Thune
Niels Juelsgt.
Solli

Nobels gate
Skarpsno
Skillebekk
Vikatorvet

Frognerkilen

A Communicarta
Style 45 design
© Communicarta Ltd 2006 UDN.1
Map user Ref:WZFG/CS/OSL/2007/012

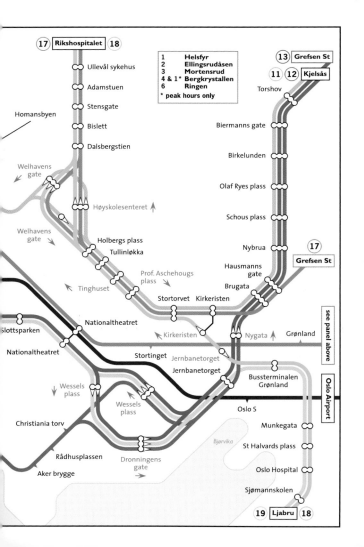

1	Helsfyr
2	Ellingsrudåsen
3	Mortensrud
4 & 1*	Bergkrystallen
6	Ringen

* peak hours only

offer lower rates, but the cars can be questionable, and they have been known to add extras charges. If you get a traffic ticket, the fine will be automatically charged to the credit card you used to hire the car. Major rental agencies include:

Avis ⓦ www.avis.no
Gardermoen Airport ⓘ 64 81 06 60
Sandefjord Airport Torp ⓘ 33 46 95 50
City ⓐ Munkedamsveien 27 ⓘ 81 56 90 44
Budget ⓦ www.budget.no
Sandefjord Airport Torp ⓘ 33 46 60 50
City ⓐ Munkedamsveien 27 ⓘ 22 01 76 10
Europcar ⓦ www.europcar.no
Gardermoen Airport ⓘ 64 81 05 60
Sandefjord Airport Torp ⓘ 33 46 42 00
City ⓐ Haakon VII Gate 9 ⓘ 22 83 12 42
Hertz ⓦ www.hertz.no
Gardermoen ⓘ 64 81 05 50
Sandefjord Airport Torp ⓘ 33 47 15 38
Oslo S ⓐ Jernbanetorget 1 ⓘ 22 10 00 0
National
Sandefjord Airport Torp ⓘ 33 47 68 00
Rent-a-Wreck ⓦ www.rent-a-wreck.no
Gardermoen Airport ⓘ 67 97 20 00
Sandefjord Airport Torp ⓘ 33 31 88 00

● *Urban city life plus fjords and mountains make for an interesting visit*

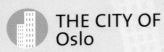
THE CITY OF
Oslo

Central Oslo

The centre of Oslo is a hive of activity, and a focal point for locals, young and old. Karl Johans Gate and the surrounding area is where you will find the greatest concentration of shops, restaurants, bars and music venues, in particular concert and opera halls. If you're more in the mood for clubs and discos, head to Rosenkrantz Gate, and for blues and jazz clubs try Stortovet.

SIGHTS & ATTRACTIONS

Aker Brygge

Once an active shipyard, this large chunk of Oslo's downtown waterfront has now been transformed into a trendy shopping and entertainment district not unlike San Francisco's Fisherman's Wharf. It's a great place to enjoy a glass of wine or a fancy dinner while taking in a panoramic view of the Akershus fortress across the water. The restaurants tend to be at the pricey end of the scale – but it won't cost you a Krone to wander the waterfront.
ⓐ Stranden 3b ⓣ 22 83 26 80 ⓦ www.akerbrygge.no
ⓜ T-bane: Nationaltheatret; Tram: 12 to Aker Brygge

Akershus Slott & Festning (Akershus Castle & Fortress)

This is probably the most striking sight in Oslo. King Haakon V ordered the construction of the fortress to protect the city after he declared Oslo the capital of Norway in 1299. Over the centuries the structure has been subject to attacks, fires, expansions, improvements and renovations. It is still under the control of

---

▶ *The impressive royal palace*

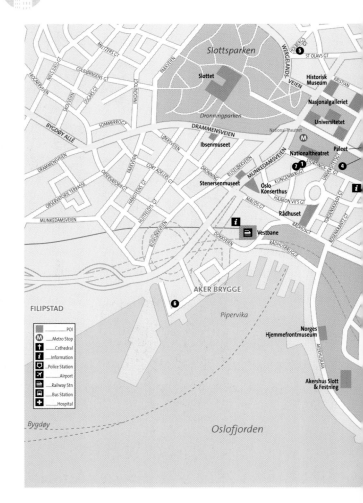

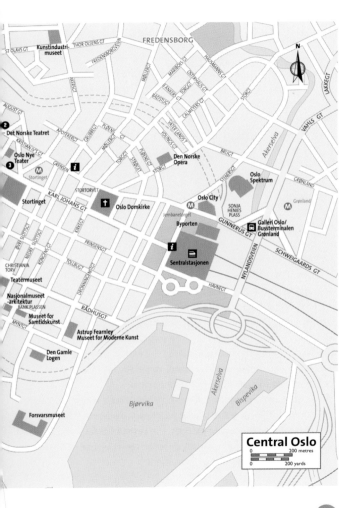

Central Oslo

| 0 | | 200 metres |
| 0 | | 200 yards |

KARL JOHAN

The King of Sweden (and Norway), known to the Scandinavians as Karl Johan, is better known to the rest of the world as Jean Bernadotte. Born of humble origins in rural France, he rose to power as one of Napoleon's marshals – and the Emperor's brother-in-law. When he was offered the crown of Sweden after the disastrous French retreat from Moscow he promptly accepted it and then led the Swedish army against his former master. A born survivor, he was the only member of Napoleon's court to establish a royal dynasty.

the military, and as such may be closed at any time for military or state functions.

The fortress is strategically located on the eastern shore of the harbour, with perfect vantage points. Gun towers were added in 1559, and for the next 200 years it was further fortified with moats and ramparts. From 1637 to 1648 it was developed into a Renaissance royal residence, and most of the luxurious state rooms, mausoleums and chapels date from this time. The crypts of Kings Haakon VII and Olaf V lie beneath the main chapel. By the early 19th century the requirement for defence was relaxed, and many of the ramparts were removed to make room for public space.

Akershus became infamous during World War II, when the Nazis took control of Norway and used it as a headquarters and as a site to execute many Norwegian patriots. The Resistance Museum, which is part of the complex, graphically describes the German occupation and the Norwegian resistance movement.

Today Akershus is one of Oslo's top tourist attractions. Aside from the lavish state rooms and chapels, the dungeons are also worth a look. There is an information centre just inside Sortieporten, and guided tours are available. The changing of the guard takes place every day at 13.30. ⓐ Akersgata ❶ 23 09 39 17 Ⓦ www.mil.no ⏱ 10.00–16.00 Mon–Sat, 12.30–16.00 Sun, May–Aug. Open in winter only for guided tours in English (13.00 Thur) Ⓝ Tram: 12 to Christiania Torv

Christiania Torv

This was Oslo's original market square, renamed with the old city name in 1958. In the 1990s the area was made vehicle-free when a tunnel was created to divert traffic. Now it's a very pleasant area, surrounded by historic buildings and filled with outdoor cafés. Markets are still occasionally held here. ⓐ Kvadraturen
Ⓝ Tram: 12 to Christiania Torv

Forsvarsmuseet (Norwegian Armed Forces Museum)

Another part of the Akershus complex is devoted to Norway's military history from the Vikings to the 1950s. Highlights include the union with Denmark and Sweden, the German invasion and the Battle of the Atlantic during World War II. The museum incorporates dioramas, models and historical objects to recreate this fascinating segment of history. ⓐ Nedre Akershus Festning ❶ 23 09 35 82 Ⓦ www.mil.no/museer ⏱ 10.00–17.00 Mon–Fri, 11.00–17.00 Sat & Sun, May–Aug; 11.00–16.00 Tues–Fri, 11.00–17.00 Sat & Sun, Sept–Apr Ⓝ Tram: 12 to Christiania Torv

Karl Johans Gate

Located in the heart of Oslo, Karl Johans Gate is the best known and liveliest thoroughfare in the city, if not the entire country.

● *Not everyone liked the City Hall's stark, modern lines when it was built*

Named after King Karl Johan, the street was designed by architect H D F Linstow in 1840 and is home to many of Norway's top institutions, such as Slottet (Royal Palace), Stortinget (Norwegian Parliament) and Nationaltheatret (the National Theatre). Lined with shops, restaurants and cafés, Karl Johan is great for shopping and eating. In winter the upper part of the street is transformed into a skating rink.

Norges Hjemmefrontmuseum (Norwegian Resistance Museum)

Housed in one of the old buildings of the Akershus fortress complex,
near the memorial on the spot where Norwegian patriots were
executed by the Germans in World War II, this museum was created
through the initiative of people who had been actively engaged in
the Norwegian Resistance. Five years of occupation from invasion
to liberation are uncompromisingly recreated through documents,
newspapers, posters, artefacts and sound recordings. ⓐ Building 21,
Akershus Festning ⓣ 23 09 31 38 ⓦ www.mil.no/museer
ⓛ 10.00–17.00 Mon–Sat, 11.00–17.00 Sun, June–Aug;
10.00–16.00 Mon–Fri, 11.00–16.00 Sat & Sun, Sept–May

Oslo Domkirke (Cathedral)

This beautifully ornate building dating from 1699 is the principal
church for the diocese of Oslo. Over the years it has undergone many
renovations and the various architectural styles are reflected in the
decorative aspects. Among some of the prominent adornments are
a stained glass window by artist Emmanuel Vigeland (brother of
sculptor Gustav Vigeland), a silver sculpture of the Lord's Supper by
Arrigo Minerbi and bronze doors by Dagfin Werenskiold. The marvellous
painted ceiling was created by Hugo Louis Mohr between 1936 and
1950. The church has played and continues to play a prominent role
in the city: in 2001 the wedding of Prince Haakon and Mette-Marit
was held here. The main parts of the church are closed for visitors
until autumn 2009 due to renovation work. ⓐ Stortorvet ⓣ 23 31 46 00
ⓦ www.oslodomkirke.no ⓛ 10.00–16.00 ⓝ Bus: 37 to Stortorvet

Rådhuset (City Hall)

Oslo's City Hall is best known as the location from which the Nobel
Peace Prize is awarded each year in December. Designed by Arnstein

Arneberg and Magnus Poulsson and opened in 1950, it is a splendid example of modernist architecture, although it was a long time before residents warmed to such a radical departure from the norm. The ceremonial main hall of the complex covers 1,519 sq m (16,350 sq ft) of space and is graced by Henrik Sørenson's oil painting, the largest in Europe, on the rear wall. **ⓐ** Fridtjof Nansens Plass **ⓣ** 23 46 81 06 **ⓦ** www.rft.oslo.kommune.no **ⓛ** 09.00–17.00 Mon–Fri, closed Sat & Sun **ⓝ** Tram: 12 to Rådhusplassen

Slottet–Det Kongelige Slott (Royal Palace)

This imposing royal residence dominates the west end of Karl Johans Gate. It was commissioned by King Karl Johan of Sweden following his ascent to the throne in 1818, after Norway had been ceded to Sweden by Denmark. The king was keen to emphasise his claim on Norway, and commissioning this palace was an important aspect of his PR campaign. Work on the elaborate neo-classical structure began in 1825 but it overran its schedule and budget; it was not completed until 1848, by which time the king had died. In fact, the palace was seldom used by the Swedish monarchs and often shut up in darkness; when the first King of Norway, Haakon, took over the palace in 1905 it was considered uninhabitable, with no running water or toilets, and Haakon was reluctant to burden the state with the expense of renovation. It was only in 1991, on King Harald's accession, that a full evaluation was carried out and the decay declared to be even worse than had been feared; the restoration costs are still controversial and work has only been partly carried out. However, some state rooms have been fully (and magnificently) renovated and are open to the public.

Tours of the interior are restricted, but normally available in summer: call for more information. The gardens surrounding the palace are always open to the public. There is a changing of the guard every day at 13.30. ⓐ Drammensveien 1 ❶ 22 04 87 00 Ⓦ www.kongehuset.no ⏰ 11.00–17.00 Mon–Thur, 13.00–17.00 Fri & Sun (also on royal birthdays, 4 July & 20 July), closed Sat, late June–mid-Aug Ⓝ T-bane: Nationaltheatret

Stortinget (Parliament Building)

Norway's National Assembly building was built in the 1860s of yellow brick and reddish granite. The assembly chamber, which seats the 165 members of parliament, was designed to resemble an amphitheatre. The building has been richly embellished, both inside and out, by various Norwegian artists; look out for the tapestry, *Solens Gang*, by artist Karen Holtsmark. Guided tours can be booked in advance. ⓐ Karl Johans Gate 22 ❶ 23 31 31 80 Ⓦ www.stortinget.no Ⓝ T-bane: Stortinget

Universitetet

The University of Oslo dominates the northeast side of Karl Johans Gate. The three buildings of the complex are in the neo-classical style and together with the National Theatre create an imposing atmosphere. The Aula, an auditorium dating from 1911, houses several murals by Edvard Munch (he considered them to be his masterpiece). Until the Rådhuset was built, the Nobel Peace Prize was presented in the Aula. ⓐ Karl Johans Gate ❶ 22 85 50 50 Ⓦ www.uio.no Ⓝ T-bane: Nationaltheatret

CULTURE

Astrup Fearnley Museet for Moderne Kunst
(Astrup Fearnley Museum of Modern Art)

Home to an extensive collection of post-war art from a large number of Norwegian and international artists, this privately owned museum opened in 1993. ❸ Dronningensgate 4 ❶ 22 93 60 60 ❿ www.af-moma.no ❺ 11.00–17.00 Tues, Wed, Fri; 11.00–19.00 Thur, 12.00–17.00 Sat & Sun, closed Mon ❿ Tram: 12, 13, 19 to Dronningensgate; Bus: 30, 31, 32, 54, 60 to Dronningensgate/Kongens Gate; T-bane: Stortinget or Jernbanetorget

Gamle Logen

This building has had many uses since its inauguration in 1839. It was here that Vidkun Quisling was sentenced to death for treason at the end of World War II. At various times in the intervening years the building has served as a place for city council meetings, a concert hall and labour office. Finally, in 1980, the Oslo Summer Opera moved in and now the building is once again being used for musical events. ❸ Grev Wedels Plass 2 ❶ 22 33 44 70 ❿ www.logen.no ❿ Tram: 12 to Christiania Torv

Historisk Museum

The Historical Museum actually comprises the three university museums, Oldsaksamlingen (National Antiquities Collection), Etnografisk Samling (Ethnographic Museum), and Myntkabinettet (Collection of Coins & Medals). Together they thoroughly document Norwegian history from the earliest settlements to the present day. ❸ Frederiks Gate 2 ❶ 22 85 99 12 ❿ www.khm.uio.no ❺ 11.00–17.00

Tues–Sun, closed Mon, mid-May–mid-Sept; 11.00–16.00 Tues–Sun,
closed Mon, mid-Sept–mid-May Ⓝ T-bane: Nationaltheatret

Ibsenmuseet

The Ibsen Museum, home of Norway's most celebrated playwright,
has been lovingly and painstakingly restored to the decoration and
furnishings of his period. Ibsen and his wife lived here from 1895 until
his death in 1906. Guided tours of Ibsen's apartment are given on the
hour. ⓐ Henrik Ibsens Gate 26 ⓣ 22 12 35 50 ⓦ www.ibsenmuseet.no
ⓛ 11.00–18.00 Tues–Sun, closed Mon, mid-May–mid-Sept; 11.00–16.00
Tues, Wed, Fri–Sun, 11.00–18.00 Thur, closed Mon, mid-Sept–mid-May
Ⓝ Tram: 13, 19 to Nationaltheatret; T-bane: Nationaltheatret

Museet for Samtidskunst (Museum of Contemporary Art)

This museum, housed in an art nouveau building, contains Norway's
largest collection of Norwegian and international post-war art. The
permanent collection is so big that only part of it is on display at any
one time. Famous works include Gunnar Gundersen's *Winter Sun* and
Per Manning's photographic portraits of animals. ⓐ Bankplassen 4
ⓣ 21 98 22 57 ⓦ www.nationalmuseum.no ⓛ 11.00–17.00 Tues,
Wed & Fri, 11.00–19.00 Thur, 12.00–17.00 Sat & Sun, closed Mon
Ⓝ Bus: 46, 37, 33 to Nordahl Bruns Gate; T-bane: Nationaltheatret

Nasjonalgalleriet (National Gallery)

Norway's National Gallery is home to the country's largest public
collection of paintings, sculptures, drawings, engravings and other
art forms. The Edvard Munch Hall contains a number of the artist's
most famous works, including the only painted version of *Skrik*
(*The Scream*) available to the public. (The other painting was stolen
from the Munch Museum in 2004. It was recovered but found to be

damaged, and is therefore not on show.) The museum also features the work of other Norwegian artists and foreign masters, including Christian Krohg, El Greco, Modigliani, Peter Blake and Harald Sohlberg. ⓐ Universitetsgata 13 ⓣ 21 98 20 00 ⓦ www.nationalmuseum.no ⓛ 10.00–18.00 Tues & Wed, 10.00–19.00 Thur, 10.00–18.00 Fri, 11.00–17.00 Sat & Sun, closed Mon ⓝ T-bane: Nationaltheatret; Tram: 11, 17, 18 to Tullinløkka

Nasjonalmuseet–arkitektur (National Museum of Architecture)

In March 2005 this museum closed its exhibition space at Kongens Gate 4. It is due to reopen in the former Bank of Norway building at Bankplassen 3 in spring 2008. The Norwegian architect of the new building, Sverre Fehn, is also designing an exhibition pavilion for the garden. ⓐ Postboks 7014, St Olavs Plass ⓣ 21 98 20 00

Nationaltheatret

Oslo's National Theatre opened its doors in 1899 with a production of Ibsen's *An Enemy of the People* and it has consistently kept the playwright's work at the core of its repertoire ever since. You'll get more than just a night at the theatre here: it houses one of the country's finest art collections, with works by Vigeland, Werenskiold, Fjell and Krohg. The baroque-style building itself is also noteworthy: it was designed by Henrik Bull and is typical of theatre architecture in Europe of the late 19th century. ⓐ Johanne Dybwads Plass 1, off Stortingsgata ⓣ 22 00 14 00, Tickets 81 50 08 11 ⓦ www.nationaltheatret.no ⓝ T-bane: Nationaltheatret; Tram: 13, 19

Den Norske Opera (Norwegian State Opera)

It wasn't until 1959 that Oslo acquired this, its first opera house. Unfortunately, this building does not have the ideal acoustics for

● *Visit the National Theatre to see Ibsen's famous plays*

operatic performances but a new opera house has now been
built, and it will open at Nylandsveien 20b, Bjørvika in April 2008.
ⓐ Storgata 23 ❶ 81 54 44 88 ⓦ www.operaen.no ⓝ T-bane: Nygata
or Storgata

Norske Teatret (Theatre of Norway)

The company was founded in 1913 but didn't have a permanent
home until 1995, when the curtain went up on this ultra-modern

construction. It is the main venue in Oslo for works in Norwegian, both classical and modern. Kristian IVs Gate 8 22 47 38 00 or 22 42 43 44 (ticket reservations) www.detnorsketeatret.no Bus: 33 to Prof Aschehougs Plass

Oslo Konserthus

Opened in 1977, the Oslo Concert Hall is home to the Oslo Philharmonic Orchestra. It is also the leading venue for concerts and musical productions in the city, with more than 300 events staged here annually. The building was specially designed to present orchestral works and the podium is large enough to accommodate 120 musicians at any one time. Munkedamsveien 14, public entrance from Ruseløkkveien 23 11 31 00 www.oslokonserthus.no T-bane: Nationaltheatret

Oslo Nye Teater (New Theatre)

Some of Oslo's more urbane and modern theatre presentations are staged here. For many years the repertoire was dominated by comedy but in recent times it has become more diverse. Productions are held at three locations: Hovedscenen in Rosenkrantz Gate, the Centralteateret in Akersgata and Trikkestallen in Thorshovgata. Rosenkrantz Gate 10 22 34 86 00 www.oslonye.no

Stenersenmuseet

The Stenersen Museum is named after author and art collector Rolf Stenersen, who in 1936 donated his entire collection to the city of Oslo. It was not until 1994 that the collection was removed from storage and placed in this new museum, along with the private collections of Amaldus Nielsen and Ludvig Ravensberg, two of Norway's more prominent 19th-century artists. The collection includes paintings and drawings by Edvard Munch, a close friend of Stenersen, Kai Fjell and Jakob Weidemann. ⓐ Munkedamsveien 15 ⓣ 23 49 36 00 ⓦ www.stenersen.museum.no ⓛ 11.00–19.00 Tues & Thur, 11.00–17.00 Wed, Fri–Sun, closed Mon ⓝ T-bane: Nationaltheatret

Teatermuseet
Housed in the former town hall, this museum traces the history of theatre in Oslo from 1800 onwards. ⓐ Christiania Torv 1 ⓣ 22 46 65 09 ⓝ Tram: 12 to Rådhusplassen

RETAIL THERAPY

The area around Karl Johans Gate is pedestrian friendly and home to shopping centres and department stores. You won't have any problem finding a souvenir or gifts.

SHOPPING CENTRES
Byporten Adjacent to Central Station, this mega-mall has more than 70 stores, including fashion, sport and toy shops. Cafés and restaurants are on hand for post-retail refreshment. ⓐ Jernbanetorget 6 ⓣ 23 36 21 60 ⓦ www.byporten.no ⓛ 10.00–21.00 Mon–Fri, 10.00–20.00 Sat, closed Sun ⓝ T-bane: Jernbanetorget or Oslo S

Oslo City Close to Central Station, with lots of fashion, book and department stores. ⓐ Stenersgata 1 ⓣ 81 54 40 33 ⓦ www.oslocity.no ⓛ 10.00–22.00 Mon–Fri, 10.00–20.00 Sat & Sun ⓝ T-bane: Jernbanetorget or Oslo S

Paleet Come here to admire the bronze statue of Norwegian skating heroine Sonja Henje, and then shop in the upmarket complex of

45 stores. Handy if the weather's bad. ⓐ Karl Johans Gate 37–43
ⓣ 22 03 38 88 ⓦ www.paleet.no ⓛ 10.00–20.00 Mon–Fri,
10.00–18.00 Sat, closed Sun ⓝ T-bane: Nationaltheatret

DEPARTMENT STORES & INDEPENDENT SHOPS

Bare Jazz Centrally located jazz café and record store that's
a treasure trove for jazz lovers. ⓐ Grensen 8 ⓣ 22 33 20 80
ⓦ www.barejazz.no ⓛ 10.00–18.00 Mon & Tues, 10.00–24.00
Wed–Sat, closed Sun ⓝ T-bane: Jernbanetorget

Galleri Format Over 300 Norwegian artists are represented at this
shop, which sells all kinds of handicrafts in all manner of materials,
including ceramic, glass, metal and wood. It's worth a look if only
to browse the art exhibitions ⓐ Rådhusgata 24 ⓣ 22 41 45 40
ⓦ www.format.no ⓛ 11.00–17.00 Tues–Fri, 11.00–16.00 Sat,
12.00–16.00 Sun, closed Mon ⓝ Tram: 19 to Kirkegata

GlasMagasinet One of the biggest department stores in Norway,
this is an excellent place to hunt down something special for your
home. It's a major outlet for Hadeland Glassverk, prime Norwegian
glassware. An excellent coffee shop and restaurant are also on site.
ⓐ Stortorvet 9 ⓣ 22 90 87 00 ⓦ www.glasmagasinet.no ⓝ Bus: 37;
Tram: 11, 17

Handelsstedet Bærums Verk Set in an ironworks dating from 1610,
this market is a good place to come for unique handicrafts. If you
get tired of shopping you can always wander the museum.
ⓐ Verksgata 1 ⓣ 67 13 00 18 ⓦ www.baerumsverk.no ⓛ 10.00–20.00
Mon–Fri, 10.00–18.00 Sat, closed Sun ⓝ Bus: 753, 143 to Bærums Verk

Norway Designs Clothes, jewellery, paper – you name it: anything with Norwegian twist can be found here. ⓐ Stortingsgata 28 ⓣ 23 11 45 10 ⓦ www.norwaydesigns.no ⓛ 09.00–17.00 Mon–Wed, Fri, 09.00–19.00 Thur, 10.00–15.00 Sat, closed Sun ⓝ T-bane: Nationaltheatret

Smykketeatret Just the place to find an original piece of jewellery by a Norwegian artist. There are also hand-crafted pieces from Indonesia, designer jewellery from Denmark, steel work from Germany and gold from Israel. ⓐ Kristian Augusts Gate 3 ⓛ 10.00–17.00 Mon–Wed, Fri, 10.00–19.00 Thur, 11.00–16.00 Sat, closed Sun, Sept–mid-May; 10.00–16.00 Mon–Wed, Fri, 10.00–18.00 Thur, 10.00–15.00 Sat, closed Sun, mid-May–Sept ⓝ Bus: 33 to Prof. Aschehougs Plass ⓣ 21 53 12 22 ⓦ www.smykketeatret.no

TAKING A BREAK

Foxx £ ❶ A trendy little coffee bar in the Hotel Continental, conveniently right next door to the National Theatre. ⓐ Stortingsgata 24–26 ⓣ 22 82 41 74 ⓦ www.hotel-continental.no ⓛ 07.30–24.00 Mon–Thur, 07.30–01.00 Fri, 10.00–01.00 Sat, 12.00–24.00 Sun ⓝ T-bane: Nationaltheatret

Hambro's Café ££–£££ ❷ One of the classiest coffee shops in the city, with subtle colours and antique furnishings. Choose from all sorts of goodies from the bakery, including filled ciabattas and luscious pastries. ⓐ Kristian IVs Gate 7 ⓣ 22 82 60 00 ⓦ www.bristol.no ⓛ 11.30–20.00 Mon–Fri, 11.30–17.00 Sat, closed Sun ⓝ Tram: 11, 17, 18 to Tinghuset

Grand Café £££ ❸ Ibsen is said to have had lunch at this café every day. It's a bit pricey, but worth it for the atmosphere – not to mention the cake buffet. ⓐ Karl Johans Gate 31 ❶ 23 21 20 18 ⓦ www.grand.no ⓛ 11.00–23.00 ⓝ T-bane: Nationaltheatret

AFTER DARK

RESTAURANTS

TGI Friday's ££ ❹ Yes, it's an American chain restaurant with predictable choices such as ribs and steaks, but it's affordable and lively. ⓐ Karl Johans Gate 35 ❶ 22 33 32 00 ⓦ www.tgifridays.com ⓛ 11.00–23.00 Mon–Wed, 11.00–23.30 Thur–Sat, 12.00–23.30 Sun ⓝ T-bane: Nationaltheatret or Stortinget

Enzo Bar & Restaurant £££ ❺ Located in the Radisson SAS Scandinavia (see page 36), this restaurant has a decent, wide-ranging menu. It's also a nice place just for a drink. ⓐ Holbergs Gate 30 ❶ 23 29 30 00 ⓦ www.scandinavia.oslo.radissonsas.com ⓛ 10.00–24.00 Mon–Sat, 11.00–20.00 Sun ⓝ Tram: 11, 17, 18 to Holbergs Plass

Lofoten Fiskerestaurant £££ ❻ The outdoor tables at this restaurant are perfect for a summer evening. The décor is modern and stylish, and the excellent fish menu changes seasonally. ⓐ Stranden 75 ❶ 22 83 08 08 ⓦ www.lofotenfiskerestaurant.com ⓛ 11.00–01.00 Mon–Sat, 12.00–24.00 Sun ⓝ Tram: 12 to Aker Brygge; Bus: 54 to Aker Brygge

Theatercaféen £££ ❼ This restaurant in the Hotel Continental opened in 1901 and, more than 100 years later, retains an authentic turn-of-the-century flair. It has been a haven for many of Norway's

● *A central pavement café awaits the throngs*

notables, including Edvard Munch and Knut Hamsun.
ⓐ Stortingsgata 24–26 ⓣ 22 82 40 50 ⓛ 11.00–23.00 Mon–Sat,
15.00–22.00 Sun ⓝ T-bane: Nationaltheatret

BARS & CLUBS

Etoile Bar Set above the city on the seventh floor of the Rica
Grand Hotel (see page 36), this charming bar is a lovely place for
a nightcap. ⓐ Karl Johans Gate 31 ⓣ 23 21 20 00 ⓦ www.grand.no
ⓛ 11.00–24.00 Mon–Thur, 11.00–01.00 Fri & Sat, closed Sun
ⓝ T-bane: Nationaltheatret or Stortinget

● *Do as Ibsen did and lunch at the Grand Café*

Luna Park With its 1970s-inspired interior, this popular club is a real step back in time. Expect long queues. ● Badstugata 1 ● 22 20 82 55 ● 15.00–03.00 Mon–Thur, 14.00–03.00 Fri & Sat, closed Sun ● T-bane: Tøyen

Onkel Donald One of Oslo's hot spots, this café-bar combines really good Norwegian food with a chic atmosphere. Late at night it changes

from an eatery to a bar. ➋ Universitetsgata 26 ➊ 23 35 63 10
Ⓦ www.onkeldonald.no Ⓛ 11.00–24.00 Mon–Wed, 11.00–03.00
Thur–Sat, closed Sun Ⓝ T-bane: Nationaltheatret

Panorama Will it be the breathtaking views or the designer martinis
that you remember the most? There's only one way to find out.
It's also worth stopping by during the day for a tapas lunch.
➋ Oslo Plaza Hotel, Sonja Henies Plass 3 ➊ 22 05 80 34 Ⓛ 13.00–01.00
Mon–Thur, 13.30–02.00 Fri & Sat Ⓝ T-bane: Jernbanetorget

Sikamikanico DJs of all types set an ever-changing tone at Sikamikanico,
one of the city's best club scenes. ➋ Møllergata 2 ➊ 22 41 44 09
Ⓦ www.sikamikanico.no Ⓛ 21.00–03.30 Wed–Fri, 13.00–03.30 Sat,
22.00–03.30 Sun Ⓝ Tram: 11, 17, 18 to Stortorvet

Spasibar Located near the Royal Palace, Spasibar attracts a mostly
younger clientele for its arty atmosphere. ➋ St Olavs Gate 32
➊ 22 11 51 90 Ⓦ www.spasibar.com Ⓛ 14.00–04.00 Mon–Fri,
20.00–04.00 Sat & Sun Ⓝ T-bane: Nationaltheatret

Summit 21 Enjoy the view along with your cocktail at this bar high
on the 21st floor of the Radisson SAS Scandinavia Hotel. ➋ Holbergs
Gate 30 ➊ 23 29 30 00 Ⓦ www.scandinavia.oslo.radissonsas.com
Ⓛ 16.00–01.00 Mon–Thur, 16.00–02.00 Fri, 16.00–02.30 Sat,
17.00–01.00 Sun Ⓝ Tram: 11, 17, 18 to Holbergs Plass

Tiger Tiger Attracts a steady stream of the young and dance-mad.
➋ Torggata 5 ➊ 98 28 32 23 Ⓦ www.oslo.tigertiger.no Ⓛ 23.00–03.30
Thur–Sat, closed Sun–Wed Ⓝ Tram: 11, 17, 18 to Stortorvet

Grünerløkka & Grønland

Two pockets of eastern Oslo have rapidly been emerging as dynamic multi-cultural areas with an impressive array of nightlife and eateries. Grünerløkka has changed from a dingy and run-down part of town, mostly home to the city's immigrants, into a trend-setting district. The cafés and restaurants have started to outgrow the area and have spilled into neighbouring Grønland. For locations, see the main city map, pages 54 and 55.

SIGHTS & ATTRACTIONS

Oslo Spektrum

A venue for big concerts, cultural and sporting events, this is where the Nobel Peace Prize Concert, the Norwegian Military Tattoo and the Oslo Horse Show are held. International artists such as Paul McCartney, Elton John and Sting also perform here when they come to town. ⓐ Sonja Henies Plass 2 ⓣ 22 05 29 00 ⓦ www.oslospektrum.no ⓝ Tram: 18, 19 to Bussterminalen Grønland

CULTURE

Kunstindustrimuseet (Museum of Applied Art)

The Museum of Applied Art, established in 1876, is one of the oldest of its kind in Europe. It houses a fine collection of Norwegian and foreign crafts and clothes from the 17th century to the present. The star of the collection is the Baldishol Tapestry, dating from 1200. This national treasure is the only surviving Norwegian tapestry that employed the Gobelin technique, and was only found when the Baldishol Church in Hedmark county was demolished in 1879.

⬥ *The Edvard Munch Museum*

The museum also contains silver, ceramics and furniture. ⓐ St Olavs Gate 1 ❶ 21 98 22 89 ⏱ 11.00–17.00 Tues, Wed, Fri, 11.00–19.00 Thur, 11.00–16.00 Sat & Sun, closed Mon ⓝ T-bane: Nationaltheatret; Bus: 33, 37, 46 to Nordahl Bruns Gate

Munch-museet (Munch Museum)

The Munch Museum houses the world's largest collection of work by Edvard Munch. Just before his death, the artist bequeathed all the paintings in his possession to the city. The collection is massive, containing some 1,100 paintings, 4,500 drawings and 17,000 prints. On display are several versions of *The Scream*, his best known work. In 2004, following the theft of one of only two painted versions of *The Scream* (as well as a Madonna), the museum was closed for months while security was upgraded. The paintings have been found and the thieves convicted, but major repairs are needed on them and it is not yet known when – or if – the artworks will ever be shown in public again. Many of Munch's other paintings are frequently on loan to other museums, but with over 180 sq m (1,937 sq ft) of exhibition space you won't feel deprived. ⓐ Tøyengata 53 ⓣ 23 49 35 00 ⓦ www.munch.museum.no ⓛ 10.00–18.00 June–Aug; 10.00–16.00 Tue–Fri, 11.00–17.00 Sat & Sun, closed Mon, Sept–May ⓝ T-bane: Tøyen; Bus: 20 to Munch Museet. Admission charge

RETAIL THERAPY

The once working-class area by the Aker River has over the last decade become one of the most interesting areas of Oslo. The atmosphere generated by so many immigrant nationalities, such as Pakistani and Somali, is both electric and eclectic. Take some time to discover the numerous small shops and delicatessens. The best hunting ground is the area near the main streets of Markveien and Thorvald Meyers Gate.

Bonaparte A little bit punk, a little bit goth, and very avant garde. Clothing for both sexes. ⓐ Markveien 59 ⓣ 22 37 60 96 ⓛ 11.00–17.00 Mon–Wed, 11.00–18.00 Thur & Fri, 11.00–16.00 Sat ⓝ T-bane: Grønland; Tram: 11, 12, 13 to Olaf Ryes Plass

Fretex Indulge in something on the wild side at this second-hand clothes store. ⓐ Markveien 51 ⓣ 22 35 59 16 ⓛ 10.00–18.00 Mon–Fri, 10.00–16.00 Sat ⓝ T-bane: Grønland; Tram: 11, 12, 13 to Olaf Ryes Plass

Sjarm A cute little store, with a bit of everything – shoes, interior design and decorations. It's also open on Sundays. ⓐ Markveien 56 ⓣ 97 61 28 66 ⓝ T-bane: Grønland; Tram 11, 12, 13: Olaf Ryes Plass

TAKING A BREAK

Hotel Havana £ ❶ A quirky little delicatessen selling lots
of exotic munchies. ⓐ Thorvald Meyersgate 36 ❶ 23 23 03 23
Ⓦ www.hotelhavana.no Ⓛ 10.00–18.00 Mon–Sat, closed Sun
Ⓝ Tram: 11, 12, 13 to Olaf Ryes Plass

Kaffebrenneriet £ ❷ A great place for a breather. Try a fresh juice,
or the coffee of the day with a brownie – always a winner. ⓐ Thorvald
Meyersgate 55 Ⓦ www.kaffebrenneriet.no Ⓛ 07.00–19.00 Mon–Fri,
09.00–17.00 Sat, 10.00–17.00 Sun Ⓝ Tram: 11, 12, 13 to Olaf Ryes Plass

QBA £ ❸ Very cool, very hip and very wired. You can use one of their
computers or access the internet via wireless connection – just try
not to drop any of the nachos, wraps or salads onto your laptop.
ⓐ Olaf Ryes Plass 4 Ⓦ www.qba.no Ⓛ 08.00–01.00 Mon–Fri,
11.00–01.00 Sat & Sun Ⓝ Tram: 11, 12, 13 to Olaf Ryes Plass

Fru Hagen £–££ ❹ A trendy, arty sort of place serving international
dishes until 21.30, when it turns into an upmarket bar. Be prepared
for a long wait for an outside table during the summer. ⓐ Thorvald
Meyers Gate 40 ❶ 22 38 24 26 Ⓛ 11.00–01.00 Mon–Thur, 11.00–03.30
Fri & Sat, 11.00–00.30 Sun Ⓝ Tram: 11, 12, 13 to Olaf Ryes Plass

Mucho Mas £–££ ❺ It doesn't look much from the outside, but the
food here is top-notch Mexican. You'll find tacos, burritos, nachos
and plenty of beer to put out the fire from too many *chiles rellenos*.
ⓐ Thorvald Meyers Gate 36 ❶ 22 37 16 09 Ⓦ www.muchomas.no
Ⓝ Tram: 11, 12, 13 to Olaf Ryes Plass

AFTER DARK

RESTAURANTS

Punjab Tandoori £ ❻ Samosas, dal and tasty curries that aren't too hot (unless you ask for them that way) make for a filling and not-too-expensive meal very near the T-bane station. ⓐ Grønland 24 ❶ 22 17 20 86 ❶ 11.00–23.00 Mon–Sat, 11.00–22.00 Sun ⓝ T-bane: Grønland

Sult ££ ❼ A highly popular and informal restaurant that's always filled with hungry diners waiting to plough into platefuls of pasta and fish. Get there early or be prepared to wait. ⓐ Thorvald Meyers Gate 26 ❶ 80 02 01 66 ⓝ Tram: 11, 12, 13 to Olaf Ryes Plass

Bistro Brocante ££–£££ ❽ An excellent choice if you're in the mood for French cuisine. In summer this Parisian-style bistro has outdoor tables, which are always at a premium. Be sure to try the coq au vin. ⓐ Thorvald Meyers Gate 40 ❶ 22 35 68 71 ❶ 11.00–23.00 ⓝ Tram: 11, 12, 13 to Olaf Ryes Plass

BARS & CLUBS

Bar Boca Call it small or intimate, this bar with its 1950s-inspired interior is without doubt one of the coolest venues in Grünerløkka. Probably the best Bloody Mary in town, too. ⓐ Thorvald Meyersgate ❶ 22 04 13 77 ⓦ www.barboca.no

Blå A hot spot for young lovers of jazz and good music in general. Hosts a mix of live music and different club nights. ⓐ Brenneriveien 9c ❶ 40 00 42 77 ⓦ www.blaaoslo.no

● *Grünerløkka's hotspot number one, Bar Boca*

Café Kaos Another addition to Grünerløkka's ever-expanding music scene. Great for the summer, with its large outside area. ⓐ Thorvald Meyers Gate 56 ⓣ 22 04 69 90 ⓦ www.cafekaos.no ⓛ 14.00–03.30 Mon–Sat, 14.00–20.00 Sun

Gloria Flames A bar with a roof garden – the perfect combination for a hot summer's night. ⓐ Grønland 18 ⓣ 22 17 16 00 ⓦ www.gloriaflames.no

Parkteateret Bar og Scene This is one of the trendiest places in town – but be prepared to queue. ⓐ Olaf Ryes Plass 11 ⓣ Club: 22 35 63 00, Bar: 93 28 80 02 ⓦ www.parkteatret.no ⓛ 12.00–01.00 ⓞ Tram: 11, 12, 13 to Olaf Ryes Plass

Bygdøy Peninsula

Bygdøy was an island until the end of the 19th century, when the sound between Frognerkilen and Bestumkilen was filled. Today this area is home to some of Oslo's finest museums and attractions. The peninsula is easy to access – just take the ferry that runs from the quay opposite the Rådhuset. There are also frequent bus connections from the city centre. In addition to cultural sights, the area is also home to meadows and parklands filled with a wealth of plant species, and in summer the beaches are a popular place to escape to .

SIGHTS & ATTRACTIONS

Frammuseet (Fram Museum)

Next door to the Kon-Tiki Museum is the Fram Museum, home of the polar ship *Fram*. Dating from 1892 and billed as 'the world's strongest ship', she has sailed to the North Pole and the far reaches of Antarctica. Used by explorers Nansen and Amundsen on their expeditions, the ship has been on display since 1936; you can board and walk round her to see the preserved objects from those great voyages. The ship and the rest of the museum house equipment, photographs and paintings, and chart the unique contribution of these and other Norwegians to polar exploration. ⓐ Bygdøynesveien 36 ⓣ 23 28 29 50 ⓦ www.fram.museum.no ⓛ 10.00–15.00 Mon–Fri, closed Sat & Sun, Jan & Feb; 10.00–16.00 Mar & Apr; 10.00–17.00 May; 09.00–18.00 Mon–Fri, closed Sat & Sun, June–Aug; 10.00–17.00 Mon–Fri, closed Sat & Sun, Sept; 10.00–16.00 Mon–Fri, closed Sat & Sun, Oct; 10.00–15.00 Mon–Fri, closed Sat & Sun, Nov &Dec. ⓥ Bus: 30 to Bygdøynes; Ferry: 91 from Rådhuskaia 3 (City Hall Quay) to Bygdøynes (May–Sept)

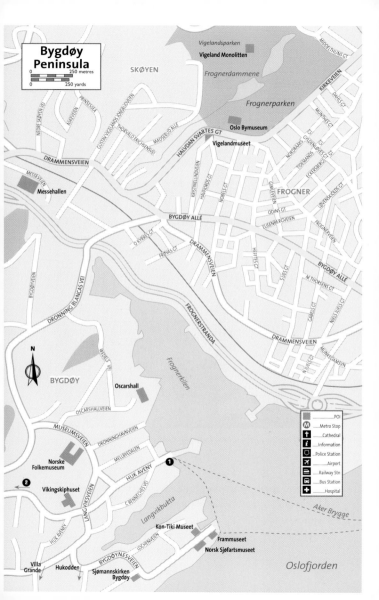

🔺 *This cart is part of the Viking heritage on display at Frammuseet*

Hukodden

This hook-shaped promontory is home to Paradisbukta (Paradise Bay), perhaps the best beach and seaside park in Oslo. Because it is easily accessible from the city, it teems with bathers on weekends. But if lying sardine-style on the beach isn't for you, there are plenty of walkways along the shore and through the adjoining woods. From the furthest point on the Huk, or 'head', you'll get a terrific view of the of the Oslofjord, stretching from the Dyna lighthouse to Nesodlandet in the south. If you prefer to sunbathe au naturel, head for the naturist beach to the north of Paradise Bay. The bay is only 15 minutes' walk from the museums of Bygdøy, and there's a restaurant on hand, too. ⓐ Strømsborgveien 46 M ❶ 22 43 74 62 Ⓝ Bus: 30 to Bygdøy Huk; Ferry: 91 from Rådhuskaia 3 (the City Hall Quay) to Bygdøynes (May–Sept)

Kon-Tiki Museet (Kon-Tiki Museum)

Thor Heyerdahl held the world's interest in 1947 when he sailed his balsawood raft *Kon-Tiki* across the vast reaches of the South Pacific to prove it would have been possible for South Americans to reach Polynesia by boat. The raft and artefacts of the voyage are on display here, at the Kon-Tiki Museum, along with exhibitions from Easter Island, including a ten-metre-high statue and a 30-metre-deep cave. There's also a short film about Heyerdahl's voyage, played on a loop. ⓐ Bygdøynesveien 36 ❶ 23 08 67 67 ⓦ www.kon-tiki.no ❶ 10.30–16.00 Jan–Mar; 10.00–17.00 Apr & May; 09.30–17.30 June–Aug; 10.00–17.00 Sept; 10.30–15.30 Oct–Dec Ⓝ Bus: 30 to Bygdøynes; Ferry 91 from Rådhuskaia 3 (the City Hall Quay) to Bygdøynes (May–Sept)

Norsk Sjøfartsmuseum (Norwegian Maritime Museum)

From the elegant ships of the early Viking explorers to the latter-day supertankers, Norway has always been at the forefront of marine activity. Completing the trio of institutions in this corner of Bygdøy is this museum displaying the history and traditions of Norwegian fishing, shipbuilding and marine archaeology. The exhibit halls feature an abundance of model ships, and the well-stocked library contains a marvellous collection of drawings, photographs and literature. ⓐ Bygdøynesveien 37 ① 24 11 41 50 ⓦ www.norsk-sjofartsmuseum.no ⓛ 10.00–18.00 Mon–Fri, closed Sat & Sun, mid-May–mid-Sept; 10.30–16.00 Mon–Fri, closed Sat & Sun, mid-Sept–mid-May ⓝ Bus: 30 to Bygdøynes; Ferry 91 from Rådhuskaia 3 (the City Hall Quay) to Bygdøynes (May–Sept)

Norske Folkemuseum (Norwegian Folk Museum)

More than 150 buildings gathered from all over Norway have been assembled here to create Europe's largest open-air museum. Wander through centuries of everyday history via farmhouses, market streets and churches; there's even a petrol station from the 1920s. The Gol Stave Church, adorned with paintings and carvings, has survived from the 12th century and is one of 30 such preserved churches in the country. Costumed guides play their roles well, while annual events include the Midsummer Eve Festival and the Christmas market in December. ⓐ Museumsveien 10, Bygdøy ① 22 12 37 00 ⓦ www.norskfolke.museum.no ⓛ 10.00–18.00 Mon–Sat, mid-May–mid-Sept; 11.00–15.00 Mon–Fri, 11.00–16.00 Sat & Sun, mid-Sept–mid-May ⓝ Bus: 30 to Bygdøy; Ferry from City Hall pier (Aker Brygge) during summer

Oscarshall

Every king needs a place to get away from it all, and 19th-century King Oscar I was no exception. This residence was originally conceived as a showcase of the architecture, art and handicrafts of the country. The castle is Norway's finest neo-Gothic building and was extensively renovated in 1929. Terraces with fountains lead down to the sea.

● *The quaint Gol Stave Church is one of the stars of the Norske Folkemuseum*

● *The Maritime and Fram Museums keep naval enthusiasts happy*

The residence is closed for renovations, but opens again in 2009.

ⓐ Oscarshallveien 805, Bygdøy ❶ 22 56 15 39 Ⓦ www.kongehuset.no
Ⓝ Bus: 30 to Kongsgården

Sjømannskirken Bygdøy (Sailors' Church)

This is the Oslo Seamen's Mission, devoted to those who work on the ships in the port of Oslo and used as a social centre. The grounds are home to the Seamen's Memorial, which was erected in 1966 to commemorate all the Norwegian sailors who have perished at sea.

ⓐ Admiral Børresens vei 4 ❶ 22 43 82 90 Ⓦ www.sjomannskirken.no
Ⓝ T-bane: Nationaltheatret; Bus: 30 to Herbernveien

Vikingskipshuset (Viking Ship Museum)

This museum houses the world's best-preserved Viking ships. Built in the ninth century, the two burial ships are an impressive sight. The museum is also home to Viking-era small boats, sledges, an ornately decorated cart and household gear. ⓐ Huk Aveny 35, Bygdøy ⓘ 22 13 52 80 ⓦ www.khm.uio.no ⓛ 11.00–16.00 Mon–Fri, closed Sat & Sun, Oct–Apr; 09.00–18.00 Mon–Fri, closed Sat & Sun, May–Sept ⓝ Bus: 30 to Vikingskipene; Ferry 91 from Rådhuskaia 3 (the City Hall Quay) to Dronningen (May–Sept)

Villa Grande

The former residence of Norwegian Nazi collaborator Vidkun Quisling has been turned in to a Holocaust centre, with a permanent

exhibition on the Holocaust and other genocides. Displays include sound, film, photos and artefacts. ⓐ Huk Aveny 56 ⓣ 22 84 21 00 ⓦ www.hlsenteret.no ⓛ 10.00–16.30 Tue–Fri, 11.00–16.30 Sat & Sun, closed Mon ⓝ Bus: 30 to Bygdøy

RETAIL THERAPY

The best bets for shopping in the Bygdøy area are the gift stores in the various museums, which are filled to the brim with Norwegian handicrafts. In December the Christmas market at the Norsk Folkemuseum is not to be missed.

TAKING A BREAK

Lanternen Restaurant £££ ❶ This restaurant is looking fresh and new after a spruce-up. The maritime surroundings make it perfect for summer. The menu changes with the season. ⓐ Huk Aveny 2 ⓣ 22 43 78 38 ⓦ www.restaurantlanternen.no ⓝ Bus: 30 to Folkemuseet

Sult Hukodden £££ ❷ This restaurant is only open during the summer season, and offers fresh seafood and tasty lunches. ⓐ Strømsborgveien 46 M ⓣ 22 43 74 62 ⓛ From 12.00, May–Sept ⓝ Bus: 30 to Bygdøy Huk; Ferry: 91 from Rådhuskaia 3 (the City Hall Quay) to Bygdøynes (May–Sept)

◀ *Heroic figureheads at the Maritime Museum*

Holmenkollen, Frogner & Majorstua

Much of what Oslo has to offer is located to the northwest of the
city centre. Whether it's the sculptures in Frogner-Vigelands Park,
the ski jump at Holmenkollen, or the many museums in the suburbs,
you'll want to allow some time to visit them. Label-conscious party
animals will feel right at home in the west-end atmosphere of
Majorstua and Frogner, while Bogstadveien and Hegdehaugsveien
have an abundance of bars and pubs that stay open long into the
night. Thankfully, Oslo's efficient public transport system makes it
easy to get to all of these places. For sights in Frogner, see the map
on page 91; other sights are on the main map, page 54.

SIGHTS & ATTRACTIONS

Bogstad Herregard (Bogstad Manor)

An 18th-century farming estate lying on the eastern bank of Bogstad
Lake, Bogstad Herregard dates back to the Middle Ages. It was owned
by a series of famous and wealthy Norwegians before becoming
an extension of the Norsk Folkemuseum in 1954. The current Manor
House was built in the late 1700s by Peder Anker, who went on to
become Prime Minister. Most of the artwork and other artefacts
date to that time, as do the beautiful English-style park and
gardens surrounding the estate. There is a café and a shop on site.
ⓐ Sørkedalen 826 ⓣ 22 06 52 00 ⓦ www.bogstad.no ⓛ 12.00–16.00
Tues–Sat, 12.00–17.00 Sun ⓥ Bus: 32 to Røa, then 41 to Bogstad

Frognerseteren

This recreational area near Holmenkollen is the starting point
for well-marked hiking and skiing trails in the Nordmarka woods.

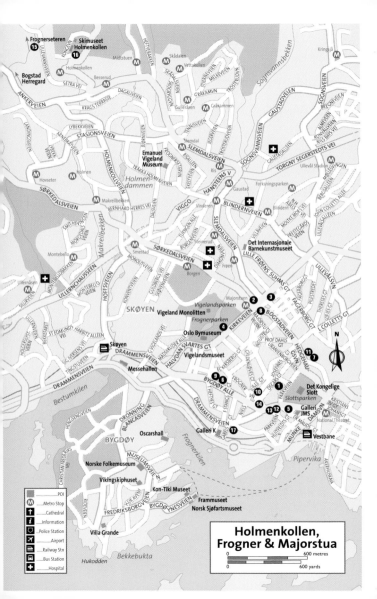

Originally inhabited in 1790, it became public at the end of the 19th century when a traditional wooden lodge was built, which now houses the restaurant. From the observation tower you can see Oslo, the Oslofjord and even Sweden. ⓐ Holmenkollveien 200 ⓣ 22 92 40 40 ⓛ 11.00–22.00 ⓝ T-bane: Frognerseteren

Holmenkollen

No stay in Oslo would be complete without a trip to this world-famous ski jump, if for no other reason than to enjoy its magnificent view of the city. The best time to come is when there's a competition on, which normally means winter. Fortunately, there are activities at Holmenkollen all year round. For a real thrill, try the ski simulator, followed by a more sedate trip to the Ski Museum or a look around the other ski-related exhibitions on site. Concerts are held in summer. There's also a restaurant and an extensive gift and souvenir shop.

The **Ski Museum** is located at the foot of the ski jump. It opened in 1923 and covers over 4,000 years of skiing history. It displays various types of skis, as well as exhibits relating to different skiing events, such as the Olympic Winter Games in Oslo in 1952 and Lillehammer in 1994. There are exhibits covering the Antarctic expeditions of Amundsen and Scott, and the Greenland expedition of Nansen. Norway's hosting of the Olympics in 1952 and 1994 is featured, too. The exhibition extends to Norwegian paintings and other artwork connected with winter activities, as well as a newly opened exhibition with a collection of photos of the Royal Family skiing. ⓐ Kongeveien 5 ⓣ 91 67 19 46 ⓦ www.holmenkollen.com and www.skiforeningen.no ⓛ 10.00–17.00 Sept–May; 09.00–20.00 June–Aug ⓝ T-bane: Holmenkollen. By car, it takes 20 minutes to get to the Holmenkollen area from the city centre: from Ring Road 3, exit at Smestad and follow the signposts to Holmenkollen. From the city centre, there are signposts from Majorstua to Holmenkollen.

◔ *You can visit the top, but take a deep breath before you look down!*

Internasjonale Barnekunstmuseet
(International Museum of Children's Art)

Founded in 1986 in association with SOS Children's Villages and featuring children's art from over 150 countries, the museum is a showcase for paintings, sculptures, ceramics, textiles and collages. Children can participate in music, dance, painting and drawing, and there are also films, videos and workshops. The on-site shop is worth a browse. ⓐ Lille Frøens Vei 4 ⓣ 22 46 85 73 ⓦ www.childrensart.com ⓛ 11.00–16.00 Tues–Thur, Sun, closed Mon, Fri, Sat, mid-June–mid-Aug; 09.30–14.00 Tues–Thur 11.00–16.00 Sun, closed Mon, Fri, Sat, mid-Aug–mid-June ⓝ T-bane: Frøen; Bus: 46

Vigelandsparken (Vigeland Park)

This large park, part of the much bigger Frogner Park, is dedicated to sculptor Gustav Vigeland and contains 212 of his works. The centrepiece is the 17 m (53 ft) high *Monolitten* (Monolith), with 121 human figures supporting each other. Other highlights are the bridge and the fountain. The park has tennis courts that are open in the summer and an adjacent public swimming pool, which is open during the summer. There's also a visitors' centre and a café at the main entrance. ⓐ Kirkeveien ⓣ 23 49 37 00 ⓦ www.vigeland.museum.no ⓝ T-bane: Majorstuen; Bus: 20; Tram: 12 to Vigelandsparken

CULTURE

Emanuel Vigeland Museum

This unusual building was once the studio of Emanuel Vigeland, the younger brother of Gustav, and is now his mausoleum as well as a museum (his ashes are in an urn over the entrance door). Although renowned for his frescoes and stained glass, Emanuel also painted and sculpted. On display here in a dark barrel-vaulted room is *Vita (Life)*, a group of frescoes that was considered very risqué when they were produced in the 1940s. ⓐ Grimelundsveien 8 ⓣ 22 14 57 88 ⓦ www.emanuelvigeland.museum.no ⓛ 11.00–17.00 Tues–Sun, closed Mon, June–Aug ⓝ T-bane: Slemdal; Bus: 46 to Grimelundsveien

Oslo Bymuseum (Oslo City Museum)

Located in the Vigelandsparken, this 18th-century manor house is dedicated to the history of Oslo, with models, pictures, room interiors and displays. There are three other buildings, which together with the museum form a traditional farm layout with an open square in the middle. A café and shop are on site, too. ⓐ Frogner Hovedgård (Frogner

● *Share Vigeland's astonishing visions at the park named after him*

Manor), Frognerveien 67 23 28 41 70 www.oslobymuseum.no
11.00–16.00 Tues–Sun, closed Mon T-bane: Majorstuen; Bus: 20;
Tram: 12 to Frogner Plass

Vigelandsmuseet (Vigeland Museum)

The museum dedicated to Norway's great sculptor Gustav Vigeland
lies just outside Vigelandsparken, and contains the majority of
the artist's work – 2,700 sculptures and 10,000 drawings, woodcuts
and carvings, to be precise. It was built in Norwegian neo-classical
style, initially as a studio for Vigeland on the understanding that
it would eventually become a museum containing his work. His
ashes are in the museum's tower. Nobelsgate 32 23 49 37 00
www.vigeland.museum.no 11.00–17.00 Tues–Sun, closed Mon,
June–Aug; 12.00–16.00 Tues–Sun, closed Mon, Sept–May
T-bane: Majorstuen; Bus: 20; Tram: 12 to Frogner Plass.

Private galleries

Galleri JMS One of the best galleries in Oslo for contemporary art,
by both Norwegian and international artists. Arbinsgate 3
22 92 55 02 www.gallerijms.no

Galleri K Owned by Ben Fria, a noted authority on the
works of Edvard Munch and many other Norwegian artists.
Bjørn Farmannsgate 6 22 55 35 88 www.gallerik.com

RETAIL THERAPY

Between the Royal Palace and Vigeland Park is the retail shopping
area of Majorstua. The best shops, many of them featuring designer
and high-end clothing, are on Hegdehaugsveien and Bogstadveien.

Frogner is also home to designer clothing shops and furniture stores. For unusual gifts and souvenirs, check out the area's museum shops.

Amalies A little clothing store stocking a well-chosen collection of high-quality Danish brands such as Ilse Jacobsen and Mind. ⓐ Bogstadveien 8 ① 22 56 67 00 ① 10.00–18.00 Mon–Fri, 10.00–19.00 Thur, 10.00–17.00 Sat, closed Sun ⓦ www.amalies.no Ⓝ T-bane: Majorstuen

🔺 *Oslo's Karl Johan street*

Anton Sport Høyfjellsutstyr This sports equipment store has Norway's biggest selection of backpacks. Norwegian brands such as Sweet, Norrøna and Ajungilak all feature. Bogstadveien 1 23 33 43 80 www.antonsport.no 10.00–18.00 Mon–Fri, 09.00–16.00 Sat, closed Sun T-bane: Majorstuen

Kamikaze Exclusive designer clothing for those who like to be on the cutting edge of style. Hegdehaugsveien 24 22 60 20 25 10.00–17.00 Mon–Wed, 10.00–18.00 Thur, 10.00–17.30 Fri, 10.00–15.30 Sat, closed Sun T-bane: Majorstuen

Lille Vinkel Sko Carries a range of young, trendy shoes. Kirkeveien 59 22 46 86 18 www.lillevinkelsko.no 09.00–18.00 Mon–Wed & Fri, 09.00–19.00 Thur, 10.00–17.00 Sat T-bane: Majorstuen

MA Noted for its exclusive designer clothing, this is the place to go if you need to dress to impress. Hegdehaugsveien 27 22 60 72 90 10.00–18.00 Mon–Fri, 10.00–16.00 Sat, closed Sun, Aug–June; 10.00–17.00 Mon–Fri, 10.00–15.00 Sat, closed Sun, July T-bane: Majorstuen

Tonica Vintage Corner As its name suggests, this store specialises in vintage clothes. Schøningsgate 14 22 60 22 06 11.00–17.00 Tues–Sat, closed Sun & Mon, late Aug–early July; 11.00–17.00 Wed, closed Thur–Tues, early July–late Aug www.tonicavintage.com T-bane: Majorstuen

TAKING A BREAK

Frogner and Majorstua offer a wide variety of cafés and restaurants, some fairly exclusive, and many catering to the young and trendy.

Åpent Bakeri £ ❶ Don't say we didn't warn you! The freshly baked bread and just brewed coffee here are simply irresistible... so don't be surprised to find a queue out of the door and down the street. ⓐ Inkognito Terasse 1 ⓣ 22 44 94 70 ⓛ 07.30–17.00 Mon–Fri, 09.00–15.00 Sat, closed Sun ⓝ T-bane: Nationaltheatret

Samson £ ❷ This traditional corner bakery-café is a nice place to stop and put your feet up for a bit in between rounds of sightseeing. ⓐ Valkyriegata 8 ⓣ 22 46 50 75 ⓦ www.samson.no ⓛ 07.30–17.00 Mon–Fri, 08.30–15.00 Sat, 11.00–17.00 Sun ⓝ T-bane: Majorstuen

Café M ££ ❸ A ten-minute walk from Vigelandsparken, this place has a bar/café area, as well as a full restaurant, plus outdoor seating in summer. ⓐ Valkyriegata 9 ⓣ 22 60 34 00 ⓦ www.cafem.no ⓛ 11.00–01.00 Mon–Sat, 12.00–24.00 Sun ⓝ T-bane: Majorstuen

Herregardskroen ££ ❹ In the Oslo Bymuseum in Frogner Park, Herregardskroen is a good place to get away from the hustle and bustle of the city. Surrounded by open space, large trees and Frogner Lake, it has good views of the park and of Holmenkollen. ⓐ Frognerveien 67 ⓣ 22 43 77 30 ⓦ www.herregaardskroen.no ⓛ 12.00–22.00 Easter–Sept ⓝ T-bane: Majorstuen

Pascal ££ ❺ Pascal's is famous for its pastries and cakes that border on being works of art. Bill Clinton stopped in to indulge in the goodies in the glass cases. ⓐ Henrik Ibsens Gate 36 ⓣ 22 55 00 20 ⓦ www.pascal.no ⓛ 09.00–24.00 Mon–Fri, 10.00–24.00 Sat, 12.00–17.00 Sun ⓝ T-bane: Nationaltheatret

Café Elise ££–£££ ❻ A cheerful and sunny little bistro with glass walls that let the light in. Limited menu, though. ⓐ Elisenbergveien 22

☎ 22 44 25 11 **🕐** 11.30–23.00 Mon–Sat, 13.30–22.00 Sun
Ⓝ T-bane: Nationaltheatret; Bus: 30 to Frogner Kirke

Lorry ££–£££ **❼** This two-storey restaurant practically doubles as a gallery, showcasing more than 270 pieces of art. The atmosphere is warm and inviting. **ⓐ** Parkveien 12 **☎** 22 69 69 07 **Ⓦ** www.lorry.no
🕐 11.00–03.30 Mon–Sat, 12.00–01.30 Sun

AFTER DARK

The Majorstua and Frogner areas of Oslo are the trendiest and most expensive parts of town. This is where you go to see and be seen. Dress your best and expect some long waits on the weekends, unless you've made reservations in advance.

Den Gamle Majors Lab £ **❽** Originally a traditional pub, now a light and hip place for Oslo's trendiest. Light meals are served.
ⓐ Bogstadveien 66 **☎** 22 46 29 04 **Ⓝ** T-bane: Majorstuen

Clodion Art Café £–££ **❾** A colourful bar/café for those interested in art and the art scene in the city. A good place to come if you have kids in tow. **ⓐ** Bygdøy Allé 63 **☎** 22 44 97 26 **Ⓦ** www.clodion.no
🕐 11.00–24.00 Mon–Sat, 11.00–22.30 Sun **Ⓝ** T-bane: Nationaltheatret

Pizza Da Mimmo £–££ **❿** It's not often that you need to make reservations for a low-budget pizzeria, but this place is the exception. This casual and cosy place serves excellent pizza: in fact, it's one of the most popular eateries in Oslo. **ⓐ** Behrens Gate 2 **☎** 22 44 40 20
Ⓝ T-bane: Nationaltheatret

● *Majorstua is a good place to go bar-hopping*

Havana Social Club ££ ⓫ Desperate smokers will find relief in the outdoor bar/pub setting of this pub. ⓐ Hegdehaugsveien 31 ⓣ 22 46 02 00 ⓦ www.havanasocialclub.no ⓛ 16.00–01.00 Mon, 16.00–03.00 Tues–Fri, 11.30–03.00 Sat, 15.00–01.00 Sun ⓝ T-bane: Nationaltheatret

Palace Grill ££ ⓬ You can't make a reservation for this small, hip restaurant, so expect a bit of a wait, while watching Oslo's trendies on parade. There's no à la carte menu, just an eight-course meal, so come hungry! ⓐ Solligate 2 ⓣ 23 13 11 40 ⓦ www.palacegrill.no ⓝ T-bane: Nationaltheatret

Amici Trattoria ££–£££ ⓭ An Italian-style place that's great for a light meal or just a drink. On Friday and Saturday it's also a nightclub. ⓐ Henrik Ibsens Gate 90 ⓣ 22 54 71 71 ⓦ www.amici.no ⓝ T-bane: Nationaltheatret

Bagatelle Restaurant £££ ⓮ Bagatelle is the only restaurant in Oslo with two Michelin stars, so be prepared to dig deep into your wallet for the gourmet food. One of Oslo's in-spots, with décor to match. ⓐ Bygdøy Allé 3 ⓣ 22 12 14 40 ⓛ 18.00–late Mon–Sat ⓦ www.bagatelle.no ⓝ T-bane: Nationaltheatret

Frognerseteren £££ ⓯ A beautiful old log building with a cosy fireplace and good views of the city, this place exudes romance. The excellent food is a further bonus. ⓐ Holmenkollveien 200 ⓣ 22 92 40 40 ⓦ www.frognerseteren.no ⓛ 11.00–22.00 ⓝ T-bane: Frognerseteren

Holmenkollen Restaurant £££ ⓰ Serving a mix of Norwegian and international dishes, the restaurant at the famous ski jump dates all the way back to 1892. Check out the views of Oslo and Oslofjord. ⓐ Holmenkollveien 119 ⓣ 22 13 92 00 ⓦ www.holmenkollen-restaurant.oslo.no ⓛ 11.00–22.00 Mon–Sat, 11.00–20.00 Sun ⓝ T-bane: Besserud

Hos Thea £££ ⓱ A warm and friendly restaurant with a large fireplace to give it that extra added glow. ⓐ Gabels Gate 11 ⓣ 22 44 68 74 ⓦ www.hosthea.no ⓝ Tram: 10 to Skillebekk

---

ⓞ *The Norwegian King's summer house in Bergen*

OUT OF TOWN
trips

Oslo fjords & Bergen

When you visit Oslo, you must take time to see the fjords. Thanks to typical Norwegian efficiency, it is unbelievably easy to take in a few fjords, some spectacular countryside and a thrilling train ride all in a neat little package called 'Norway in a Nutshell', which can be booked as a package (see Ⓦ www.visitnorway.com).

As it leaves Oslo the train sweeps out of the city and across the country's mountainous spine, with its forests, lakes and glaciers. Not surprisingly, this route was recently voted one of the world's most beautiful. The railway was completed in 1909 and is considered to be an engineering feat. It's 300 miles long and has some 300 bridges and 200 tunnels, all of which you will journey past in less than seven hours.

At Myrdal, a 12-mile spur line plunges down 900 m (2,800 ft) in just under an hour, to Flåm. This handy little town is really little more than a whistle stop for the train. You'll want to make a connection to Aurland, a charming country village a few miles north, whose speciality is *geitost* (goats cheese). If your train ride into Flåm hasn't satisfied your need for mountain scenery, take the train to Berkvam and hike or bike the gravel road back down to Flåm. Be sure to bring a picnic.

From Flåm most 'nutshellers' catch one of the fjord cruises. Be prepared for 90 minutes of non-stop camera clicking as tourists scurry back and forth across the boat decks in quest of the perfect photo. The fjord walls are so close you'll feel as though you could reach out and touch them. Most boats travel up the narrow Aurlandsfjord and then down the Nærøyfjord to Gudvangen, where buses will shuttle you to the town of Voss. At Voss it's time to hop the train and proceed to Bergen, Norway's second city and historic capital.

You can finish the day there by browsing the touristy waterfront area, taking a harbour ferry, or zipping up the funicular to the top of the 320 m (1,000 ft) tall Mount Fløyen for a view of the city. All too soon it's time to catch the overnight train back to Oslo. In just 24 hours you will have experienced the mountains, fjord and countryside of Norway – in a nutshell.

But don't think you can't spend a little longer in any of those places, above all Bergen.

SIGHTS & ATTRACTIONS

Although it's famous for its wooden buildings at the Hanseatic wharf in old Bryggen, Bergen has a lot more to offer. Billing itself as the 'Gateway to the Fjords', it is a historical international city with small-town charm. In the late Middle Ages it was the most populous and

BERGEN CARD

The Bergen Card gives free admission to most museums, free travel on local buses and the Fløibanen funicular (see page 120) and free guided tours of Bergen, as well as reduced prices for other attractions, concerts and boat tours. It also includes free parking, so if you have a car, the card will almost pay for itself in parking fees. The card is available for 24 and 48 hour periods and can be purchased from the local tourist office, railway station, bus terminal and some hotels. Lower-price cards are available for children aged 3–15.

● *Bergen takes its name from the hills which rise directly behind it*

most important city in Norway. Among later claims to fame, it was the home of composer Edvard Grieg.

Bryggen

Designated a UNESCO World Heritage site, Bryggen is famous for its pretty wooden buildings with pointed gables facing the harbour. The area dates back to the 14th century, when Bergen joined the Hanseatic League and became a major northern trading centre. The Bryggens Museum displays artefacts uncovered in archaeological digs from 1955 to 1972, and also shows the foundations of the city's oldest buildings on the original site. The chance to dig came after a disastrous fire in 1955 burned many of the buildings. Excavations under the burned ruins uncovered over a million items, including proof that the area had burned many times, from as early as 1170. **Bryggens Museum** ⓐ Dreggsalmenning 3 ⓣ 55 58 80 10 ⓦ www.uib.no/bmu ⓛ 10.00–17.00, May–Aug; 11.00–15.00, Sept–Apr

Håkonshallen (Haakon's Hall)

This medieval castle was built by King Haakon Haakonsson in the mid-13th century, when Bergen was the political centre of Norway. The castle was badly damaged in World War II but has been extensively restored. ⓐ Bergenhus Festning ⓣ 55 31 60 67 ⓛ 10.00–16.00, mid-May–Aug; 12.00–15.00, Sept–mid-May

Hanseatiske Museum & Schøtstuene

This is one of the best-preserved wooden buildings in Bergen. Built in 1704, it is furnished to look like the home of a Hanseatic merchant in the 18th century. Schøtstuene is an offshoot of the museum, comprising a collection of old Bryggen buildings. **Hanseatic Museum** ⓐ Finnegårdsgaten 1a ⓛ 09.00–17.00 (summer);

11.00–14.00 Tues–Fri, 11.00–16.00 Sun, closed Mon & Sat (winter).
Schøtstuene ⓐ Øvregaten 50 🕐 10.00–17.00 (summer); 11.00–14.00 Sun,
closed Mon–Sat (winter) 📞 55 54 46 90 🌐 www.museumvest.no
Admission charge

Mariakirken (St Mary's Church)

This is the oldest building in Bergen; an outstanding Romanesque
church, it was built of stone early in the 12th century. The pulpit
was donated by Hanseatic merchants in 1676, and is considered an
excellent example of baroque decorative art. ⓐ Dreggen 15 📞 55 31 59 60
🕐 09.30–11.30, 13.00–16.00 Mon–Fri, closed Sat & Sun, mid-June–Aug;
11.30–12.30 Tues–Fri, closed Mon, Sat, Sun, Sept–mid-June

Rosenkrantztårnet (Rosenkrantz Tower)

The tower was built in the 1560s by Erik Rosenkrantz, governor of
the city. It served as both a residence and as a fortified tower for
Bergen and incorporated earlier fortifications. Guided tours only.
ⓐ Bergenhus Festning 📞 55 31 43 80 🕐 10.00–16.00, mid-May–Aug;
12.00–15.00, Sept–mid-May

THE HANSEATIC LEAGUE

This alliance of powerful German trading cities arose in the
Middle Ages and long monopolised the profitable trade in raw
materials between Scandinavia, the Baltic states and northern
Europe. Its outposts reached as far as Riga and Tallinn, and
Bergen was its northernmost trading station. Hanseatic
merchants lived a rigid, monk-like existence, forbidden to
marry or dwell outside their trading colony.

Views from above

There are wonderful panoramas to be enjoyed from the surrounding hills, which can be reached by funicular or cable car. Fløibanen is a funicular that takes you up 320 m (1,000 ft) to the top of Mount Fløyen, where you get a great view of Bergen. There are several hiking trails at the top, including one that lets you walk back down to the city. Ulriksbanen is a cable car takes you up 640 m (2,100 ft) to the top of Mount Ulriken, where there is a café, radio tower, hiking trails and a spectacular panoramic view of the city and surrounding fjords. In summer double-decker buses leave from Torgalmenningen 1 to the foot of Ulriken.

Fløibanen ⓐ Vetrlidsalmenning 21 ❶ 55 33 68 00 🕒 07.30–24.00 May–Aug; 07.30–23.00 Mon–Thur, 08.00–23.00 Fri & Sat, 09.00–23.00 Sun, Sept–Apr

Ulriksbanen ⓐ Ulriken 1 ❶ 55 20 20 20 🅦 www.ulriken.no 🕒 09.00–21.00 Apr–Oct (weather permitting); closed Nov–Mar

CULTURE

Bergen Kunstmuseum (Bergen Art Museum)

This museum includes several collections, as well as paintings by Munch and Picasso. The adjoining Bergen Kunsthall features changing art exhibitions. ⓐ Rasmus Meyers Allé 3, 7 & 9 ❶ 55 56 80 00 🅦 www.bergenartmuseum.no 🕒 11.00–17.00 mid-May–mid-Sept; 11.00–17.00 Tues–Sun, closed Mon, mid-Sept–mid-May

---

▶ *Take the Fløibanen for breathtaking views of Bergen*

Bergen Museum

De Naturhistoriske Samlinger (Natural History Collections) is
a botanical garden with a partially restored old zoological collection.
There are also geological and botanical exhibits. De Kulturhistoriske
Samlinger (Bergen Cultural History Collections) range from antiquity
through the middle ages and up to the present day. Included
are archaeological finds, textiles, historical documents and an
ethnographic collection. **t** 55 58 21 49 **w** www.bergenmuseum.uib.no
b 10.00–15.00 Tues–Fri, 11.00–16.00 Sat & Sun, Sept–May;
10.00–16.00 Tues–Fri, 11.00–16.00 Sat & Sun, June–Aug
De Naturhistoriske Samlinger **a** Museplass 3 **t** 55 58 29 49
De Kulturhisoriske Samlinger **a** Haakon Sheteligsplass 10 **t** 55 58 31 40

Bergens Sjøfartsmuseum (Bergen Maritime Museum)

Like its counterpart in Oslo (see pages 93–4), this museum tells the
story of Norwegian shipping from early times to the present day.
Established in 1921, it has a collection of models of Viking ships and
other working boats. **a** Haakon Sheteligs Plass 15 **t** 55 54 96 00
b 10.00–18.00 Mon–Fri, 11.00–16.00 Sat & Sun, June–Aug;
11.00–16.00 Mon–Fri, 12.00–16.00 Sun, closed Sat, Sept–May

Grieghallen

Bergen's concert hall – and Norway's largest auditorium – is named
after its most famous citizen, composer Edvard Grieg. The Bergen
Philharmonic Orchestra, founded in 1765, performs here every
Thursday evening from September to May. **a** Edvard Griegs Plass 1
t 55 21 61 00 **w** www.grieghallen.no

Kulturhuset
This former sardine factory has been converted to Bergen's main cultural centre, with a full range of contemporary arts such as music, film, dance and theatre. ⓐ Georgernes Verft 12

Den Nationale Scene (Norwegian National Theatre)
Founded in 1850 by Ole Bull, Bergen's famed violinist, the theatre is housed in a landmark art nouveau building. Henrik Ibsen was a director here between 1851 and 1857. ⓐ Engen 1 ⓣ 55 54 97 00 ⓦ www.den-nationale-scene.no

Norges Fiskerimuseum (Norwegian Museum of Fisheries)
Established in 1880, this is the oldest museum of its type in Norway. Displays show natural resources, management and products of the fishing industry that is still a major element in Norway's economy. ⓐ Bontelabo 2 ⓣ 55 32 12 49 ⓛ 10.00–18.00 Mon–Fri, 12.00–16.00 Sat & Sun, June–Aug; 10.00–16.00 Mon–Fri, 12.00–16.00 Sat & Sun, Sept–May

Vestlandske Kunstindustrimuseum (West Norway Museum of Decorative Art)
This museum has several permanent collections, as well as changing exhibits. The museum features one of the world's oldest and most beautiful violins, dating back to 1562. It was played by Norwegian virtuoso Ole Bull, another illustrious musical son of Bergen. ⓐ Nordahl Bruns Gate 9 ⓣ 55 33 66 33 ⓦ www.vk.museum.no ⓛ 11.00–17.00 mid-May–mid-Sept; 12.00–16.00 Tues–Sun, closed Mon, mid-Sept–mid-May

RETAIL THERAPY

A trading centre for centuries, Bergen continues the tradition today, with everything from small specialist shops to large department stores and malls.

Bergen Steinsenter Jewellery, watches, and objects made of stone and minerals are the draw here. A good place to find an original ornament or gift. ⓐ Bredsgarden Bryggen ⓣ 55 32 82 60

Bergen Storsenter Home to more than 70 stores, this is the biggest shopping centre in Bergen. Services include a pharmacy and a dentist. ⓐ Stromgaten 8 ⓣ 55 21 24 70 ⓦ www.bergenstorsenter.no ⓛ 09.00–21.00 Mon–Fri, 09.00–18.00 Sat, closed Sun

Bryggen Husflid A/S This sweater specialist carries a wide range of brands, including Dale of Norway, Nordstrikk and Skjæveland. It's also a popular choice for souvenirs such as woodcarvings and trolls. ⓐ Bryggen 37 ⓣ 55 32 88 03

Elg A small shop specialising in moose of varying sizes, shapes and materials. ⓐ Holmedalsgården 1 ⓣ 55 21 51 00

Galleriet This shopping mall with over 70 outlets caters to most needs. Clothes, books, cafés, a pharmacy, souvenirs and art galleries are all here. ⓐ Torgallmenningen 8 ⓣ 55 30 05 00 ⓦ www.galleriet.com ⓛ 09.00–21.00 Mon–Fri, 09.00–18.00 Sat, closed Sun

---

▶ *Bryggen carries on Bergen's centuries-old commercial traditions*

Glass Thomsen A specialist in glass, crystal, dinner sets and gift articles. They have skilled staff and good service. ⓐ Liamyrane 15 ⓣ 55 53 94 50

Julehuset The Christmas Shop is a year-round stop-off for a yule-related gift or decoration. Don't miss the large selection of typical *nisser* (Norwegian Santa Clauses). ⓐ Holmedalsgården 1 ⓣ 55 21 51 00

Kløverhuset Norway's oldest shopping centre stocks the latest fashions, with the emphasis on upmarket and trendy lines. ⓐ Strandgaten 13–15 ⓣ 55 55 88 22 ⓦ www.kloverhuset.com ⓒ 09.00–20.00 Mon–Fri, 09.00–18.00 Sat, closed Sun

Nilssen på Bryggen Conveniently located along the wharf, next to the Hanseatic Museum, Nilssen på Bryggen focuses on all things woollen, with a wide range of knitwear, wool, textiles and embroidery. ⓐ Bryggen 3 ⓣ 55 31 67 90

Ruben's Varme Gleder For a bit of fun, check out this toy and game store. Educational materials also feature, while costumes and souvenirs round out the stock. ⓐ Vetrlidsalmenning 5 ⓣ 55 31 41 11

Viking Indulge your inner Viking here. Among the Viking-related souvenirs are replicas of swords found in Viking graves (although you probably won't be able to take them back in your luggage). ⓐ Holmedalsgården 1 ⓣ 55 21 51 00

TAKING A BREAK

Baker Brun £ Don't leave Bergen without trying a *skillingsbolle* (cinnamon bun) from this little bakery at Bryggen.
ⓐ Damsgårdsvei 109a ⓣ 98 29 34 49

Søstrene Hagelin £ This seafood place opened in 1929 and is still serving up dishes the same way today. Be sure to try the fish soup. You can eat in or take away for a picnic. ⓐ Olav Kyrresgate 33
ⓣ 55 32 01 12

Dr Livingstone Travellers Café £–££ As the name hints, this place features a menu of foods from around the globe. The outdoor seating area is nice in warm weather. Great coffee bar, too.
ⓐ Kong Oscarsgate 12 ⓣ 55 56 03 12

Kløver Kafe £–££ Sit on the top floor of Kløverhuset (see page 126) and take in the view while enjoying traditional Norwegian dishes or coffee and cakes at reasonable prices. ⓐ Strandgaten 13–15
ⓣ 55 62 54 58 ⓦ www.kloverhuset.com

Kafe Kippers USF ££ This café at the Kulturhuset is a gathering spot for local artists and arty types. The Friday live jazz sessions are renowned. The on-site outdoor restaurant, Kaien, is one of Bergen's largest, with a view of the city fjord. ⓐ Georgenes Verft 3 ⓣ 55 31 00 60

Terminus Kafe ££ This continental-style café is great for sandwiches and cakes, although it also does hot dishes. ⓐ Zander Kaaesgate 6
ⓣ 55 21 25 00

AFTER DARK

RESTAURANTS

Zachariasbryggen Restauranter ££–£££ Right in the heart of the historic wharf area, this outdoor restaurant is a great place to soak up the local atmosphere. Norwegian food and a good selection of local beers. ⓐ Torget 2 ① 55 55 96 40

▶ *Nightfall in Bergen, with its many clubs and bars*

Bryggens Tracteursted £££ Another highly rated restaurant at Bryggen, this place offers a modern twist on traditional Norwegian food. ➋ Bryggestredet 2 ➊ 55 31 59 55

Fløyen Restaurant £££ Originally opened in 1925, this distinctive eatery at the top of Mount Fløyen offers an expansive menu. The views are amazing: be sure to ask for a window seat when you make the (necessary) reservation. ➋ Fløyfjellet 2 ➊ 55 31 90 30

BARS & CLUBS

Fincken-Café Bergen's only café for the gay and lesbian crowd is gets really busy at the weekend. ➋ Nygårdsgaten 2a ➊ 55 32 13 16

Fotballpuben Probably the most popular football pub in Bergen. Especially lively on nights when the local team, Brann, is playing. ➋ Vestre Torggate 9 ➊ 55 33 66 66

Garage Bergen's number one rock club caters to a twenty- and thirtysomething crowd. ➋ Christies Gate 14 ➊ 55 32 19 80 ➍ www.garage.no

Hulen Rockclub Not your average club: this one is situated in a cave. ➋ Olaf Ryes vei 48 ➊ 55 33 38 38

Metro The place to come if you want to dance to the latest hits. Remember to dress up. ➋ Nedre Ole Bulls Plass 4 ➊ 55 90 19 60

Rick's Café og Salonger Drinking and dancing are the attractions at this large club, which hosts both DJs and live concerts. ➋ Øvre Ole Bulls Plass 9 ➊ 55 55 31 31

▶ *Bergen city from the top of Fløyen*

The Scotsman This two-storey bar, with a piano bar in the basement, attracts a mainly younger clientele at weekends. ⓐ Valkendorfsgate 1b
ⓣ 55 55 87 75

Wessel Pub For decades this has been one of the most popular pubs in Bergen. Informal and always packed to the rafters.
ⓐ Ole Bulls Plass 6 ⓣ 55 90 07 39

ACCOMMODATION

Scandic Bergen City ££ A modern conference-style hotel with large and comfortable rooms. **ⓐ** Håkonsgaten 2 **ⓣ** 55 30 90 80 **ⓦ** www.scandic-hotels.no/bergencity

Augustin Hotel ££–£££ Bergen's oldest family-run hotel integrates modern amenities with good old-fashioned service. Rooms are comfortable, and some have harbour views. **ⓐ** C Sundtsgate 22–24 **ⓣ** 55 30 40 00 **ⓦ** www.augustin.no

Best Western Hotel Hordaheimen £££ In the heart of the city, very close to the railway station. **ⓐ** C Sundtsgate 18 **ⓣ** 55 21 23 00 **ⓦ** www.bestwestern.com

Comfort Hotel Holberg £££ This well-located hotel, with recently renovated rooms, is named after 18th-century poet Ludvig Holberg, who was born in a house on the site. It also boasts a health club with sauna, steam bath and solarium. **ⓐ** Strandgaten 190 **ⓣ** 55 30 42 00 **ⓦ** www.choice.no

Thon Hotel Rosenkrantz £££ A traditional hotel with excellent service. **ⓐ** Rosenkrantz Gate 7 **ⓣ** 55 30 14 00 **ⓦ** www.thonhotels.com

Hurtigruten

Everyone's image of Norway focuses on the fjords that slice deeply into its western shore, creating one of the world's most spectacular coastlines. In this northern region, the midnight sun can be seen from late May to mid-July. From September to April the Northern Lights perform brilliant shows in the dark sky, although daylight hours are very short: from mid-November to mid-January the sun never rises.

Beautiful fjord scenery is just one reason for taking the legendary coastal voyage by steamer on Norway's Hurtigruten line. The name translates as 'fast route' and these ships were once the only connection between Norway's northern coastal towns. Today's modern vessels still provide vital local transport, but are also popular for their views: from almost any place on the ships passengers can watch the changing panorama of mountains, islands, fjords and little fishing harbours. For an outline of the route, see the map on page 115.

While day passengers can use the ships to take them to remote coastal towns and islands, most travellers take the entire route, either from Bergen to Kirkenes or vice versa. Some make the trip both ways, because the ship makes daytime stops on the southbound trip where it stopped at night on the way north. An added attraction is a visit to the stunning Geirangerfjord on summer northbound sailings. Optional excursions are reasonably priced, often leaving the ship at one stop and travelling overland to re-board at a later port. Especially worthwhile are those to the North Cape, Vesterålen and Lofoten.

▶ *Stop at beautiful Trondheim on your way to the northern fjords*

Port stops vary from 15 minutes to several hours. In Vardø passengers follow a costumed drummer to the octagonal Vardohus Fort, built in the 1700s, for sea views and tours of the fort's historic buildings. In Stokmarknes the Hurtigruten Museum recalls the service's founding here in 1893. Ålesund, where the ship stops at night on its southern voyage, is worth staying up for. Its art nouveau centre is floodlit and only a short walk from the dock. One of the attractions of the Norwegian Coastal Voyage is its flexibility. The ships sail all year, departing every day. Options range from cruise-only six-day trips from Kirkenes to Bergen, to 17-day packages that combine a 12-day return-trip with days to explore Bergen and Oslo. Schedules and bookings can be made via Ⓦ www.hurtigruten.com.

SIGHTS & ATTRACTIONS

Hammerfest

This small city was levelled in World War II, when it was the headquarters for the German fleet in the North Atlantic. The crypt of Hammerfest Church was the only structure to survive, and one entire end wall of the striking rebuilt church is now a stained glass window. A museum of the reconstruction, Gjenreisningsmuseet, explores the forced evacuation of Hammerfest and the Germans' 'scorched earth' policy in the region during World War II, as well as the town's struggle to rebuild its homes and community after the war. The Royal & Ancient Polar Bear Society is a favourite stop for its small displays recording Hammerfest's relationship with this arctic creature as well as its history since the 1600s as a centre for traders from Russia, the Arctic and as far away as southern Europe. You can become a member, earning the right to wear the club emblem.
Gjenreisningsmuseet for Finnmark og Nord-Troms Ⓐ Kirkegata 21,

Hammerfest ☎ 78 42 26 30 ⓦ www.museumsnett.no/
gjenreisningsmuseet ⓛ 09.00–16.00 Mon–Fri, 10.00–14.00
Sat & Sun, mid-June–mid-Aug; 11.00–14.00 mid-Aug–mid June
Royal & Ancient Polar Bear Society ⓐ Hamnegata 3, Hammerfest
☎ 78 41 31 00

Harstad, Vesteralen

Hurtigruten passengers on the Coastal Express can opt for a shore
excursion to explore the scenic Vesterålen region by land, stopping
at the medieval Trondenes Church in Harstad. Its unusual rood screen
holds a painted pulpit, and the three altars have polychrome carved
wooden statues. Also worth a visit is the Trondenes District Museum,
telling the story of the area from the Viking period and Middle Ages
to World War II, with signage in English. Recent history is even more
vividly told on a hill above town, where in a completely restored
fortification is the enormous Adolf Gun, the world's largest land-
based gun, built by the Germans in World War II. The small islands,
connected by ferries, form a major agricultural area famed for its
pungent strawberries, which ripen in August.
Vesteralen Reiseliv (Tourist Office) ⓐ Kjøpmannsgata 2, Sortland
☎ 76 11 14 80 ⓦ www.visitvesteralen.com
Trondenes District Museum ⓐ Harstad ☎ 77 01 83 80 ⓛ 11.00–17.00
mid-June–mid-Aug; 11.00–17.00 Sun, closed Mon–Sat, mid-Apr–
mid-June, mid-Aug–Oct

North Cape

Europe's northernmost point is more than simply a geographical
landmark. The continent ends here with a bang, in a sheer drop into
jagged rocks and crashing waves. Fog frequently envelops the cape,
and in the early morning of a summer day sun plays with fog to

create a constantly changing land- and seascape. The glass-enclosed Nordkapphallen (North Cape Hall) has exhibits describing local wildlife and the dramatic story of the World War II Battle of North Cape. If you have a taste for champagne then don't miss the world's northernmost champagne bar.

Nordkapphallen ⓐ Honningsvåg ⓣ 78 47 70 30
ⓦ www.visitnorthcape.com

Tromsø

Walk straight up the hill from the harbour to reach the busy main street, Storgata, which is kept lively by the city's large student population. Almost untouched by World War II, Tromsø retains the largest collection of 19th-century wooden buildings north of Trondheim. Look out in particular for the group known as Skansen, near the harbour.

There are plenty of other sights in Tromsø. The Polar Museum in the heart of the old town is a preserved 1830s customs building housing low-tech exhibits on polar exploration. Polaria, a multi-faceted discovery centre: learning experiences centre around polar regions, with films, sea aquarium, live seals and polar research exhibits. The Arctic Botanical Garden is a good introduction to the flora of this harsh region. Visitors interested in local Sami, prehistoric and Viking culture, as well as the nature and history of northern Norway, should spend an hour or two at the outstanding University Museum. It includes some of the many ancient rock carvings found nearby, and the Viking area has a full-sized replica Viking longhouse. Finally, to appreciate the city's splendid setting between the mountains and sea, ride the Fjellheisen cable car up to Storsteinen, 380 m (1,200 ft) above.

Tourist Office ⓐ Kirkegata 2 ⓣ 77 61 00 00 ⓦ www.destinasjontromso.no
ⓛ 09.00–16.00 Mon–Fri, 10.00–14.00 Sat, closed Sun, Sept–late May;

08.30–18.00 Mon–Fri, 10.00–17.00 Sat & Sun, late May–Aug

Polaria ⓐ Hjalmar Johansensgate 12 ⓣ 77 75 01 00 ⓦ www.polaria.no
ⓛ 10.00–19.00, mid-May–mid-Aug; 12.00–17.00 mid-Aug–mid-May

Polar Museum ⓐ Søndre Tollbugate 11 ⓣ 77 68 43 73
ⓦ www.polarmuseum.no ⓛ 11.00–17.00, Mar–mid-June,
mid-Aug–Sept, mid-Oct–Dec; 10.00–19.00, mid-June–mid-Aug;
11.00–15.00 Oct–mid Oct; 11.00–15.00 Jan & Feb

Arktisk-alpin Botanisk hage (Arctic Botanical Garden)
ⓦ www.uit.no/botanisk ⓝ Bus: 20 to the university in Breivika

Universitetsmuseet Tromsø (Tromsø University Museum)
ⓐ Lars Thørings Veg 10 ⓣ 77 64 50 00 ⓦ www.tmu.uit.no
ⓛ 09.00–18.00 June–Aug; 09.00–15.30 Mon–Fri, 12.00–15.00 Sat,
11.00–16.00 Sun, Sept–May

Fjellheisen cable car ⓐ Sollivn 12 ⓣ 77 63 87 37 ⓦ www.fjellheisen.no
ⓛ 10.00–01.00 Mon–Fri, closed Sat & Sun, Apr–Sept; closed Oct–Mar

Trondheim

The main attractions of Trondheim are the beautiful Nidaros Cathedral
and walking through the streets lined with old houses. The earliest
parts of the cathedral date from 11th century, and the statues in the
spectacular façade surrounding the rose window date from the Middle
Ages to the 1980s. Highlights include the magnificent organ in the
north transept and the St Olaf painted altar front (1300). The world's
first bicycle lift, near Gamle Bybro, the picturesque 1618 bridge, saves
cyclists the long climb to Kristiansten Fort. More than 60 historic
buildings form Trøndelag Folk Museum, among them a stave church
from 1170.

Trondheim Activum (Tourist Office) ⓐ Torget, Trondheim ⓣ 73 80 76 60
ⓦ www.visit-trondheim.com ⓛ 09.00–16.00 Mon–Fri, 10.00–14.00
Sat (winter); longer in summer

Trøndelage Folkemuseum (Trøndelag Folk Museum) @ Sverresborg, Trondheim ✆ 73 89 01 00 ⓦ www.sverresborg.no ⏱ 11.00–18.00 Mon–Fri, closed Sat & Sun, June–Aug; 11.00–15.00 Mon–Fri, 12.00–16.00 Sat & Sun, Sept–May 🚌 Bus: 8

RETAIL THERAPY

Blåst Glasshytta Visit this glassblowing workshop to see beautiful glassware being made. @ Hansensgate 4, Tromsø ✆ 77 68 34 60 ⓦ www.blaast.no ⏱ 10.00–17.00 Tues–Fri, 10.00–15.00 Sat, closed Sun & Mon

Galleri Nordnorge The local artists' association operates this permanent gallery of the Festival of North Norway. Along with paintings and drawings are fine crafts. @ Normannsgata 1A, Harstad ✆ 77 02 62 51 ⓦ www.gallerinn.no ⏱ 12.00–15.00 Tues–Sun, closed Mon

Gjenreisningsmuseet This museum shop sells crafts, including hand-made candles, along with books and souvenirs. @ Kirkegata 21, Hammerfest ✆ 78 42 26 30

Perlehuset For creative souls this shop is worth a visit. Buy beads and pearls in any shape and colour to create your own jewellery. @ Jomfrugata 17B, Trondheim ✆ 73 52 43 49

Royal & Ancient Polar Bear Society The little gift shop is the perfect place to buy furry white toy bears for kids, as well as books and souvenirs relating to the Arctic and polar bears. @ Rådhusplassen 1, Hammerfest ✆ 78 41 31 00

TAKING A BREAK

Gjenreisningsmuseet Cafeteria £ Freshly made waffles, coffee, hot chocolate and cakes are served in the Reconstruction Museum's neat little café. ⓐ Kirkegata 21, Hammerfest ❶ 78 42 26 30 ⓦ www.museumsnett.no/gjenreisningsmuseet ❹ 09.00–16.00 Mon–Fri, 10.00–14.00 Sat & Sun, mid-June–mid-Aug; 11.00–14.00 mid-Aug–mid-June

Kaffistova £ Home-style Norwegian cooking in a casual restaurant-café. ⓐ Rik Kaarbosgate 6, Harstad ❶ 77 06 12 57 ❹ 08.00–18.00 Mon–Fri, 09.30–16.00 Sat, 12.00–17.00 Sun

Mormors stuer £–££ A friendly café with an old-fashioned interior. ⓐ Nedre Enkeltskillingsveita 2, Trondheim ❶ 73 52 20 22

AFTER DARK

Look to swinging Tromsø for nightlife, although its nickname 'the Paris of the North' may be an exaggeration. Storgata is where the action is – and you can forget dress codes: the small coastal town's nightlife is mostly low-key. In terms of cuisine, you might see some unusual menu choices, such as seaweed, seagull eggs and seal lasagne!

RESTAURANTS

Hells Kitchen ££–£££ An American-style eatery that's owned by the same people as the Barometer bar next door. ⓐ Storgata 30, Tromsø ❶ 77 68 25 50 ⓦ www.hells-kitchen.no

Restaurant Kompasset ££–£££ Traditional Norwegian dishes using, where possible, locally produced ingredients. ⓐ North Cape Hall, Honnigsvåg ⓣ 78 47 68 60

Ørens Kro £££ This 1863 tavern keeps its cosy old-time atmosphere, while being a popular meeting place for young professionals who work in the riverside neighbourhood. Drinks, light dishes and an à la carte dinner menu. ⓐ Dokkgata 8, Trondheim ⓣ 73 60 06 35 ⓦ www.orens-kro.no ⓛ 15.30–01.00 Mon–Sat, closed Sun

Peppermøllen £££ Fish tops the menu at this traditional restaurant, a favourite with locals. Students love the restaurant's 'brown café' for its light meals (from the same excellent kitchen) and good espresso. ⓐ Storgata 42, Tromsø ⓣ 77 68 62 60 ⓛ 17.30–22.00 Mon–Thur, 17.30–22.00 Fri & Sat, closed Sun

BARS AND CLUBS
Bryggerie Billed as 'the northernmost microbrewery in the world', this place has a DJ, live music or karaoke at weekends. ⓐ Nordkappgata 1, Honningsvåg (North Cape) ⓣ 78 47 26 00 ⓛ 10.00–02.00 Mon–Sat, closed Sun

Rick's Café The hottest spot in Trondheim, this bar/nightclub offers different club nights. ⓐ Nordregate 11, Trondheim ⓣ 73 54 65 00

ⓞ *A reminder of Viking ships on Bygdøy's waterfront*

Directory

GETTING THERE

By air

SAS Braathens have code-sharing flights to Gardermoen serving no less than eight UK cities – Aberdeen, Birmingham, Edinburgh, Glasgow, Leeds, London (City, Gatwick and Heathrow), Manchester and Newcastle – as well as Dublin in the Republic of Ireland. Similar arrangements between SAS Braathens and major European and US airlines offer flights from many US cities. British Airways fly direct to Gardermoen from London Heathrow, and from London Stansted there are also direct flights on Norwegian Airlines.

Ryanair connects the UK to Oslo Sandefjord Torp from London Stansted, Glasgow Prestwick and Liverpool.

SAS Braathens Ⓦ www.sasbraathens.no
British Airways Ⓦ www.ba.com
Norwegian Airlines Ⓦ www.norwegian.no
Ryanair Ⓦ www.ryanair.com

Many people are aware that air travel emits CO_2, which contributes to climate change. You may be interested in the possibility of lessening the environmental impact of your flight through Climate Care, which offsets your CO_2 by funding environmental projects around the world. Visit Ⓦ www.climatecare.org

By road

Oslo can be reached by car by using Highway E18 from the east or west, or Highway E6 from the north or south. With the opening of the Øresund bridge between Sweden and Denmark, it is now possible to reach Norway from the Channel ports without using a ferry. The roads in Norway are generally in good condition and well maintained, especially those in and around Oslo. If travelling in winter, check the road conditions before you leave. The wearing of seatbelts is mandatory, as is the use of headlights at all times of day. Children 12 years and younger must ride in the rear seat. Driving under the influence of alcohol is not tolerated, with the legal limit being 0.02 per cent; prison sentences and large fines are common.

The minimum age for driving is 18 years, and drivers must have a full national driving licence or an International Driving Permit (IDP). Vehicles entering Norway must have proof of registration and proof of insurance. Speed limits on highways are 80–100 kph (50–60 mph), in cities 50 kph (30 mph), with some residential areas 30 kph (18 mph). Speed limits are rigorously enforced, speed traps are abundant and the fines are high, so watch your speed.

By rail

All international trains arrive at and depart from Oslo S. A direct journey from the UK by rail will involve a cross-Channel ferry or the Eurostar to Brussels as the first leg of the journey. From London (Waterloo International) to Oslo S takes 24–30 hours, via Brussels, Cologne, Hamburg, Copenhagen and Malmö or, with fewer changes of train, via Brussels, Cologne, Copenhagen and Göteborg (Gothenburg). The monthly *Thomas Cook European Rail Timetable* has up-to-date schedules for international train services to Oslo and many Norwegian domestic routes.

Eurostar Reservations (UK) ☏ 08705 186186 ⓦ www.eurostar.com
Thomas Cook European Rail Timetable ☏ (UK) 01733 416477;
(USA) 1 800 322 3834 ⓦ www.thomascookpublishing.com

By water

DFDS sails from Newcastle to Stavanger, Bergen and Haugesund on Tuesdays and Fridays. DFDS ferries also depart from Newcastle on Sundays but only for Stavanger. In all cases the trip is an overnight one. ⓦ www.dfds.co.uk ⓣ (00 47) 21 62 13 40

ENTRY FORMALITIES
Documentation

Citizens from the EU and most English-speaking countries can visit Norway for up to three months without a visa. If arriving by car, drivers must have a national driving licence, or an International Driving Permit (see above). Licences must be carried at all times, as well as car registration documents and a valid certificate of insurance.

MONEY

Norway is not a member of the EU and has kept its traditional currency, the Norwegian Krone (Kr, usually shown in foreign exchange listings as NOK). The Krone is made up of 100 Øre. Some shops, especially in the tourist areas, may take euros and US dollars, but this is not common practice. Banks, ATMs and currency exchange kiosks are found throughout Oslo. Major credit cards are honoured at most shops and restaurants, as are euro, US dollar and UK sterling traveller's cheques.

HEALTH, SAFETY & CRIME

By international standards, Norway is a very healthy and safe country. Health standards are high; the water is safe to drink and the food safe to eat, although you might want to stay clear of *lutefisk* (see page 26).

The biggest health concerns are flu and colds in winter, and sunburn and insect bites in summer. If you plan on hiking in the great outdoors, it would be wise to be vaccinated against tick-borne encephalitis.

Norway is a member of the European Economic Agreement, and thus has free reciprocal health agreements with all EU countries. Those that qualify need to carry their EHIC card. The Norwegian Health Plan does not cover other nationals, but some countries' plans may cover all or part of medical costs in Norway, so visitors should check on this before departing. The costs of health care in Norway are quite reasonable compared to other Western countries, but non-EU visitors should carry adequate travel health insurance, and it is recommended even for visitors from within the EU.

Local pharmacies and medical centres can give advice and sell medications for most minor ailments. The majority of medical professionals in Norway speak good English.

The crime rate in Oslo is low, and it is considered one of the safest capital cities in the world. However, normal precautions should be taken to avoid pickpockets, purse snatchers and other petty criminals. Oslo has a growing drug problem, so beware of addicts, drunks and beggars. Police officers are easily identified by their black boots and trousers (trousers have a chequered trim), light blue shirts, and black caps with a police crest. Police cars and police stations are clearly marked POLITI. The police are normally unarmed, and are very friendly, helpful and courteous, so do not hesitate to ask them for information or directions. Cars should be locked and parked in open or well-lit areas, with any valuables such as jewellery, cameras, mobile phones and computers locked in the boot or otherwise out of sight.

OPENING HOURS

Banks are open Monday–Friday, usually 08.15–15.00, except Thursday, when they stay open until 17.00. Most shops operate Monday–Saturday, normally 10.00–17.00. On Thursday they stay open until 19.00, but on Saturdays they close early at 14.00. Supermarket hours are 09.00–21.00, except Saturday, when they close at 18.00. Restaurants generally open for breakfast (where served) 08.00–11.00, for lunch 12.00–15.00 and for dinner 18.00–23.00. Most museums open at 11.00 and close at 17.00, unless otherwise stated in this book. Some open earlier in the day, especially in summer.

TOILETS

Norway has Western-style toilets. Public toilets can be found at shopping malls, railway stations and bus stations, but in most cases you will have to pay up to 10Kr to use them. A few restaurants still charge to use the facilities, although most do not. Toilets at libraries and museums are normally free.

CHILDREN

Travelling with kids in Norway is quite easy. Many restaurants offer children's menus, with lower prices, hotels take a kindly attitude to travelling families, and there are plenty of sights that kids will love. Don't miss the International Museum of Children's Art (see page 103), which houses children's art from 180 countries. Holmenkollen (see pages 100–2), the most visited tourist attraction in Norway, is another favourite with young visitors. Climb to the top of the ski jump tower, tour the ski museum, have lunch in the cafeteria and visit the souvenir shop. The Norwegian Folk Museum (see page 94) is Norway's largest open-air museum, with more than 140 buildings from all around the country. You can stroll the streets of 17th-century village, peek inside a 12th-century church or roam the grounds of a 19th-century farm. If you book in advance the museum will also arrange Norwegian evenings of folk tales and folk dancing. And of course, no family visit to Oslo would be complete without a trip to Akershus Castle (see pages 62–6), with its dungeons and banquet rooms. There's even a drawbridge at the entrance.

When the weather's hot, head for the beach. The Bygdøy Peninsula has two popular beaches, Huk and Paradisbukta, which can be easily reached by bus (see pages 92–9). Another good day trip is TusenFryd, an amusement park about 10 km (6 miles) south of Oslo on Highway E6. It has rides, including carousels and roller coasters, as well as swimming and a fantasy farm. The TusenFryd bus departs from the Galleriet Oslo bus terminal up to nine times daily from 09.30 to 16.00.

If you're in town on Constitution Day, 17 May, you're in luck. Though not exactly a holiday specifically for children, it comes close. It's dedicated to families and children, and in Oslo it's celebrated with a Children's Parade and light-hearted, family-oriented activities such as games and face painting.

COMMUNICATIONS
Internet
There are lots of internet cafés in Oslo, including one at the main railway station ⓣ 22 17 19 40, which also has scanning and printing facilities. Some libraries also have access: Deichmanske Bibliotek (Municipal Library) (ⓐ Arne Garborgs Plass 4), offers 30 minutes of free access; however, you will need to call ahead to reserve a time (ⓣ 23 43 29 00).

Phone

The telephone system in Norway is very good, and quite extensive. Norway uses eight digit numbers with no area codes. Long-distance rates in Norway are among the lowest in the world. Local calls from hotel rooms and pay phones cost 5Kr. Newsstands, post offices and railway stations sell telephone cards (TeleKort). Some pay phones accept credit cards. Faxes can be sent or received from most major hotels, although it is much cheaper to send them from a post office. 900/1800 MHz mobile phones will work in Norway. Norwegian SIM cards are available, but the instructions are in Norwegian, so you might want to purchase the card directly from Telehuset, who will connect you when you buy it. Cards are also available at 7-Eleven stores and some Narvesen kiosks. Cards start at 200Kr, with 100Kr worth of calls.

To call Norway, dial your home country's international exit code (usually 00), then Norway's country code, 47, plus the eight digit number. To call internationally from Norway, dial 00 plus your own country's access code and then the area code and number (in UK area codes, omit the initial 0). Country codes include: UK 44, Republic of Ireland 353, USA and Canada 1, Australia 61, New Zealand 64 and South Africa 27.

Telehuset Ⓦ www.telehuset.no

Post

The postal service in Norway is very good. Mail going to other parts of Europe takes 2–3 days, to North America about a week. Postage for letters and postcards to other parts of Europe costs about 10Kr, and to the rest of the world about 12Kr. Post offices normally open 09.00–17.00 weekdays, 09.00–13.00 Saturdays; some offices in Oslo stay open longer. Norway also has lots of small post offices inside grocery stores, which keep the same hours as the stores.

ELECTRICITY

Norway uses 220 V, 50 Hz alternating current. Sockets take the standard continental plug with two round prongs. British visitors will need a plug adaptor for appliances; other visitors, including from North America, will also need a transformer for the different voltage. Both items are best purchased at home before travelling.

SMOKING REGULATIONS

Restrictive anti-smoking laws have been in force in Norway since June 2004. In general, smoking is not allowed in any public place or on any public transport. Smoking is not allowed in restaurants, bars and pubs, even in outdoor areas if they face other public places. Many hotel rooms are now designated as non-smoking.

TRAVELLERS WITH DISABILITIES

Norway caters for travellers with disabilities better than most countries, and all new buildings are required to have wheelchair access. Most street crossings have ramps or low curbs, and crossing signals also produce audible sounds (long beeps mean that it's safe to cross, and short beeps indicate that the signal is about to change). Many trains have spaces for wheelchairs. If you travel with a wheelchair have it serviced before your departure and carry any essentials you may need for repairs. It is also a good idea to travel with any spares of special clothing or equipment that might be difficult to replace.

However, Oslo can still be a challenge for travellers with disabilities. The Norwegian Association for the Disabled is a good source of

information on hotels, restaurants and tourist attractions that
are equipped to receive disabled visitors. Tourist offices also
can be especially helpful in determining if there is suitable
accommodation in the area you wish to visit if you make your
request in advance.

It's a good idea to double-check any information you receive,
as some establishments will advertise services that are still
to be implemented. Associations dealing with your particular
disability can be excellent sources of information on conditions
and circumstances in other countries. The following contacts
may be helpful:

Access-able Travel Source Ⓦ www.access-able.com

Australian Council for Rehabilitation of the Disabled (ACROD)
ⓐ 33 Thesiger Court, Deakin ACT 2600 ① 02 6283 3200
Ⓦ www.acrod.org.au

Disabled Persons Assembly (DPA) ⓐ 4/173–175 Victoria Street,
Wellington, New Zealand ① 64 4 801 9100 Ⓦ www.dpa.org.nz

Europe for All Ⓦ www.europeforall.com

Irish Wheelchair Association ⓐ Blackheath Drive, Clontarf, Dublin 3
① 01 818 6400 Ⓦ www.iwa.ie

Norwegian Association for the Disabled ⓐ Folke Bernadottes vei 2,
Oslo ① 22 95 28 60 Ⓦ www.nhf.no

RADAR ⓐ 12 City Forum, 250 City Road, London EC1V 8AF ① 020 7250
3222 Ⓦ www.radar.org.uk

Society for Accessible Travel & Hospitality (SATH) ⓐ 347 5th Avenue,
New York, NY 10016, USA ① 212 447 7284 Ⓦ www.sath.org

TOURIST INFORMATION

Oslo Tourist Office has branches conveniently located at Oslo S, the main railway station, and by the Rådhus (City Hall). It deals only with Oslo, and also sells Oslo Passes and can arrange accommodation. ☎ 81 53 05 55 (call centre, 09.00–16.00 Mon–Fri, closed Sat & Sun) Ⓦ www.visitoslo.com

Oslo S ⓐ Trafikanten Service Centre, Oslo-S, Jernbanetorget 1 🕐 07.00–20.00 Mon–Fri, 08.00–20.00 Sat & Sun, May–Sept; 07.00–20.00 Mon–Fri, 08.00–18.00, Oct–Apr

Rådhuset ⓐ Fridtjof Nansens Plass 5 (entrance on Roald Amundsens Gate) 🕐 09.00–16.00 Mon–Fri, closed Sat & Sun, Jan–Mar, Oct–Dec; 09.00–17.00 Mon–Sat, closed Sun, Apr, May, Sept; 09.00–19.00 June–Aug

The Oslo Promotion Tourist Office is located near the Rådhus (Town Hall). The office publishes a guide to Oslo, and a monthly brochure, *What's On in Oslo*. It has good maps of the city and the transit system. The website is quite extensive. ⓐ Fridtjof Nansens 5 ☎ 24 14 77 00 Ⓦ www.visitoslo.com 🕐 09.00–16.00 (winter); longer hours in summer

Norwegian Tourist Board Its website is very comprehensive, with lots of practical information. Ⓦ www.visitnorway.com

Norway Post This paper's website gives up-to-the-minute Norwegian news in English. The emphasis is on culture and travel. Ⓦ www.norwaypost.no

Emergencies

EMERGENCY TELEPHONE NUMBERS
Ambulance & other medical emergencies ☎ 113
Fire ☎ 110
Police ☎ 112
City Police ☎ 02800 or 22 66 90 50

MEDICAL SERVICES

Doctors

If you become ill or injured while in Norway, your hotel can refer you to a local doctor (most of them speak English). If you are not staying at a hotel, call the national 24-hour emergency medical number ☎ 113

Accidents

Oslo kommunale legevakt (Public emergency ward) ⓐ Storgata 40 ☎ 23 48 70 00 ⓦ www.legevakten.oslo.kommune.no ⓛ 24 hours daily, including public holidays ⓜ Tram/bus: Hausmanns Gate

Pharmacies

Pharmacies are open during normal shopping hours, and some are also open weekends and evenings for emergencies. If you become ill during a trip, the staff at your hotel will normally be able to put you in touch with a local doctor or the emergency medical service. If you use any prescription drugs, be sure to bring enough to last for your entire stay. Norwegian pharmacies are not permitted to give out medicine on prescriptions from outside the country, and if you do run short, you will need to contact a Norwegian doctor in order to

get a prescription for a new supply. There is a 24-hour pharmacy
near the main railway station:

Jernbanetorvet Pharmacy ⓐ Jernbanetorget 4B ⓣ 23 35 81 00
ⓦ www.vitus.no ⓛ 24 hours daily, including public holidays
ⓝ Tram: Jernbanetorget or Oslo S

Dental emergencies

Tannlegevakten Oslo's public emergency dental clinic in the city centre.
Not possible to make appointments – show up in person. For children
and adults. Minimum fee: 411Kr for a ten-minute consultancy.
ⓐ Schweigaardsgate 6 ⓣ 22 67 30 00 ⓛ 19.00–22.00 Mon–Fri,
11.00–14.00, 19.00–22.00 Sat & Sun

POLICE

Oslo Police District ⓐ Politihuset, Grønlandsleiret 44
ⓣ 02800 or 22 66 90 50

EMERGENCY PHRASES

Help!   Hjelp!   *Yehlp!*

Call an ambulance/Call a doctor/Call the police!
Ring etter en sykebil/Ring en lege/Ring politiet!
Ring ehtterehn sewkerbeel/Ring ehn lehger/Ring pulitee-er!

Can you help me please?
Kan du hjelpe meg, kanskje?
Kern doo yehlper meh, koonsher?

LOST PROPERTY
Police ☎ 22 66 98 65
Trams, buses, T-bane (Oslo Sporveier) ☎ 22 08 53 61
Railway (NSB–Oslo Central Station) ☎ 81 56 83 40

Reporting lost or stolen credit cards:
American Express ☎ 80 06 81 00
Diners Club ☎ 21 01 50 00
Eurocard ☎ 21 01 50 00
Entercard (for Visa and Mastercard) ☎ 21 31 66 00

EMBASSIES & CONSULATES
There is no Australian embassy in Oslo – Australian citizens should contact the embassy in Denmark at Dampfaergevej 26, Second Floor, Copenhagen DK-2100 ☎ +45 7026 3686 Canada
📍 Wergelandsveien 7, Oslo ☎ 22 99 53 00

South Africa Embassy 📍 Drammensveien 88 c, Oslo ☎ 09 47 2327 3220
United Kingdom Embassy 📍 Thomas Heftyes Gate 8, Oslo
☎ 23 13 27 00
United States Embassy 📍 Drammensveien 18, Oslo ☎ 22 44 85 50

▶ *The Hurtigruten sweeps through magnificent fjord scenery*

INDEX

WHAT'S IN YOUR GUIDEBOOK?

Independent authors Impartial up-to-date information from our travel experts who meticulously source local knowledge.

Experience Thomas Cook's 165 years in the travel industry and guidebook publishing enriches every word with expertise you can trust.

Travel know-how Contributions by thousands of staff around the globe, each one living and breathing travel.

Editors Travel-publishing professionals, pulling everything together to craft a perfect blend of words, pictures, maps and design.

You, the traveller We deliver a practical, no-nonsense approach to information, geared to how you really use it.